© EDITIONS ESKA 1997
ISBN 2-86911-491-5

Editions ESKA - 5, avenue de l'Opéra - 75001 Paris
Tél : 01 42 86 55 73 - Fax : 01 42 60 45 35

Information Technology -
a new path to creativity in education

An analysis of projects underway in European primary schools

Janice Richardson

in a framework-concept created by **Daniel Deberghes**

*Based on a study conducted at the request of the **AMPERE Group** and financed by the European Commission.*

...To my children, who taught me the true meaning of creativity

"Imagination is more important than knowledge"
Albert EINSTEIN

FOREWORD

« It is in Education that the great secret of human nature's perfection lies. »

KANT

The mastery of information represents one of the major challenges to be addressed by Europe. It is not merely a question of technological evolution or functional assistance, but rather the emergence of a new sociological phenomenon (the need for almost instantaneous information) and the contraction of time and space, enabling autonomy in decision-making and action, cohesion and also the preservation of Europe's social and cultural characteristics.

As a result of the economic, social and demographic changes characterising our societies, it is imperative that we make available permanent and more flexible education and training opportunities for the individual in the framework of a continuum between Education and Training.

Above all, it is necessary to develop form early childhood onwards the capacity, not just to learn, but to use a hypothetical-deductive « research » mode of reasoning which will enable each and every one of our citizens to be better prepared to face the events life brings. Today, Information Technology can help teachers in this fundamental pedagogical approach.

It is the responsibility of all the key players concerned – states, private enterprise, schools, universities and regions – to include these orientations among their own priorities, bearing in mind that improving the quality of human beings is the first element likely to liberate a new energy of creativity, innovation and adaptation to the changing realities of a universe crossed by multiple forces. A determined promotion of all the capabilities of our millions of men, women and young people will enable each of us to exorcise the fear of an uncertain future and valorise the opportunities available and the skills from which we will benefit, without clutching vainly at the past.

The present publication not only underlines the social importance of this new challenge, it also gives us an insight into what is already being done in Europe. It highlights the role man must play in our society to construct a zone of peace and thereby « escape the bondage of humanity and avoid falling back into a bondage of generations » (Victor Schoelcher).

Janice Richardson, Daniel Deberghes and the Ampere Group have, through their abnegation and their convictions, laid another vital foundation stone in the construction of our Europe. I thank them and extend my sincere congratulations.

Jacques DELORS
President of the European Commission (1985-1995)
President of the UNESCO International Commission
for Education in the 21st Century

ACKNOWLEDGEMENTS

Without the collaboration and co-operation of the teachers and experts whose names are given in the "List of those consulted or interviewed" (see Annex), this study would not have been possible. I would like to express my gratitude to each and every one of them.

In all four corners of Europe specialists and non-specialists are striving to adapt the educational system to meet the demands of the Information Age, brought about by the profound transformations that have taken place in information processing methods over the past few decades and resulting in a radically different relationship between man and information. Daniel Deberghes' combat in this field began thirty years ago with the initiation of re-training schemes for textile workers in the north of France; today it continues with his conception for the framework of the present study. I would like to express my gratitude to him for the help and guidance he has unsparingly provided throughout the past two years. I would also like to thank Alice Fracchia, at the European Commission in Brussels, and Philippe Cochinaux, Department of Law and Philosophy at the Université Catholique de Louvain, for making this study possible.

The rich discussions that have taken place at the Ampère Group meetings have largely contributed to the realisation of the present publication, in particular I would like to thank José Rebelo, author of the preface, Luxembourg Minister of Education Erna Hennicot-Schoepges and Yves Franchet at Eurostat in Luxembourg. Thanks also to Pier-Giacomo Sola in Italy, Wolff Paprotté in Germany and Ana-Maria Correia in Portugal for the meetings they set up with teachers and institutions in their respective countries.

Acknowledgement is given for permission to use documentation provided by the PRINT team in the Netherlands, NCET and Imagination Technology in Great Britain, SCRIPT in Luxembourg, the EPI association and Colette Girardot in France, Tommy Isaksson in Sweden, Eurydice in Brussels and the Ministry of Cultural Affairs in North-Rhine-Westphalia, Germany.

The most vital contribution has, of course, been made by the primary school teachers I was fortunate enough to encounter throughout the course of this project. I wish them every success in their present and future projects. I have included at the end of this publication the two grids that have been used throughout the Ampère study in the hope that more teachers will be encouraged to contribute to a future issue on this subject.

TABLE OF CONTENTS

PREFACE

The Knowledge Age is presently in a state of gestation. We recognise that existing educational methods and structures are inappropriate to this new age, and that it is therefore necessary to respond positively to the challenge. Even educationalists and specialists cannot readily agree on a solution, but we desperately feel that it is urgent to act.

This profound transformation must involve every citizen, every corporation, every association and every government.

The new information technologies are defining a new relationship between people, modifying the way of living and working. We cannot avoid the invasion of sophisticated systems into the learning process: they will promote respect and accommodate human differences, allowing all citizens to realise their full potential at their own speed.

For this reason, the Ampère Group's contribution to the process was initiated with the present study concerning the utilisation of Information Technology in primary schools.

Let us hope that this work, together with many other similar efforts, will trigger the explosion of energy necessary to create a long-needed "revolution".

J. REBELO

General Director, PETROFINA S.A.

Chairman of the Groupe Ampère

Member of the European Round Table (E.R.T.)

THE MESSAGE
FROM ANDRÉ-MARIE AMPÈRE

"Perfect myself and Man, this has always been my inspiration: I can neither work, nor feel, nor create anything that does not seek this goal."[1]

André-Marie AMPÈRE

Ampère the man who, starting out with a single observation recorded by Orsted in Denmark and transcribed by his friend Arago, discovered the second fundamental interaction of the Universe in just 9 days: **electromagnetism**, the technological applications of which have given birth to computing and telecommunications.

...the man, the very first, to inscribe to Kant's philosophy on noumenon by adopting a hypothetico-deductive form of reasoning - which to this very day remains the international method of research.

...the man who contemplated Nature and thought, above all things, of the diffusion of knowledge in harmony with Nature.

...the man with a caring heart who chose to live humbly, in poverty, in harmony, filled with the gift of abnegation and self-sacrifice.[2]

...the man who discovered the second fundamental force of the universe that today allows for the dissemination of knowledge and has opened up a new path to knowledge and **research reasoning methods**.

The late French President François Mitterrand paid tribute to André-Marie Ampère in a ceremony held at the Cité des Sciences in Paris on the occasion of the 150th anniversary of his death:

"I can discern, in your regard, your aspirations; we share the common desire that Ampère's signal endure the passage of time and be handed on to our kin, so that once again it may rekindle the vocations needed by France and its institutions. Above all, the desire that we and our people come to understand that herein lies our destiny."

He may rest assured that Ampère's message is being propagated and is, in keeping with his wish, enabling us to lead the European Union towards a society that is more just, more social, more competitive, more united, more creative... in short, more radiant... in a world which, more self-confident in its soul, has become a little more humane for all of its children.

Daniel DEBERGHES
Member of the *Société André-Marie Ampère*

INTRODUCTION

In 1995/96, at the request of the AMPERE Group, the European Union launched a twelve-month study to examine the ways in which Information Technology can be used to enhance the teaching/learning process and contribute to developing the basic knowledge, skills and strategies that will enable tomorrow's generation to become independent lifelong learners capable of assuming an active role as fully-fledged citizens in European democracy. This study led me into schools and teacher training colleges of eight European countries: Belgium, France, England, Germany, Italy, Luxembourg, Portugal, and Sweden. It was decided at the outset that attention should be focused in particular on the lower to middle classes of the primary school, since it is at this age that children are laying the vital foundation stones upon which the edifice of lifelong learning is built. Indeed, it is in these early years of primary education, at the very stage when the fundamental mechanisms governing the organisation of behaviour and thought are being established, that every effort should be made if we are to succeed in identifying and developing a child's full potential and hence counteract the negative effects of the growing social ills that are undermining our societies in today's world. Before setting out on our educational journey through Europe, we shall first make a sweeping tour of the panorama in terms of the child, the school and new insights into the learning process.

Children "inherit" their adaptation and learning capacities and strategies through a cultural transmission mechanism that takes place within their immediate environment, the first mediators of this process being family, friends and neighbours. If, for various reasons, the family has not been able to provide the mediation expected of it (pre-, peri- or post-natal deficiency, disturbed family relationships, cultural transplantation due to migration, etc.), if it refuses to do so (anti-conformism, asocial environment, etc.), if, in short, the child suffers from a "cultural gap" (some even speak of "cultural deprivation") when first going to school, then learning difficulties will necessarily occur[1]. Primary education is therefore particularly important in that it very often represents a

1. Council for Cultural Co-operation: School Education Division, *Innovation in Primary Education*, Strasbourg, Council of Europe, 1988, p.7-8

child's first encounter with mediators (teachers and peers) of a wider socio-professional environment and hence provides a new opportunity for children who have not yet developed the necessary decoding instruments for understanding and adapting their behaviour to the wider context of school and society. It is in this initial phase of education that a pupil's weaknesses and strengths emerge; only if learning impairments and difficulties are dealt with in early years can the educational system fulfil its role in providing equal opportunities for all future citizens.

Schools traditionally hold a dual role in society: on the one hand, they are an agent of change and social mobility and, at the same time, they act as a repository of the "sound roots of culture" and are responsible for handing down our heritage[2]. But today education has been brought to a cross-roads by the momentum of changes that have taken place both in Information Technology and in our understanding of the learning process. The spread of information and communication technologies has broadened the traditional gap between school and society by making our everyday lives more complex and volatile, and hence represents one of the fundamental factors that are changing the structure of the family and society. Children now have access to a whole range of information sources and channels in addition to formal education; they are inundated by such large doses of "culture" handed out by the media that if the school is to succeed in "handing down the sounds roots of culture" it must work towards developing new skills that will enable our future citizens to distinguish culture from the mass of information so readily available, to discriminate between the virtual and the real world. To renew the alliance between the school and a society in which more than 2 out of 3 employees spend a major part of their time processing information[3], the tools that have become commonplace in both work and leisure must be integrated into the learning process.

Educational research has, since the 1950's, proved beyond doubt that a child's mind is not a recipient to be filled at all cost with a maximum amount of knowledge in the form of facts and details communicated through demonstration and imitation, through words and explanation. It is now generally accepted that "elementary training" implies giving a child a basic knowledge of the essential phenomena of life and society (and of their interrelations) and the attitudes and skills that will enable him to adapt to and learn efficiently in any new situation. Through the works of Piaget, Vygotsky and many other researchers in the field of education, we have become aware that meaningful learning occurs only if children have developed a need to learn irrespective of

2. Council for Cultural Co-operation: School Education Division, *Innovation in Primary Education*, Strasbourg, Council of Europe, 1988, p.7
3. Baudé J., Rapports d'activités et orientations pour 1995-96, in *La Revue de l'association EPI*, December 1995, N°80, p.22

subject matter, or of any situational variables, qualifications or even sanctions.[4] Three vital links exist between the process of intellectual development and the acquisition of knowledge: the mechanisms for the learner's **interaction** with the whole of his environment, recognition and strengthening of the **independence** a learner needs when building up his own stock of knowledge (and assimilating school and social rules) and **assessment** designed and experienced as a formative tool and a guide to proficiency.[5]

In this study, we have set out to discover through classroom observations in primary schools in Europe, to what extent Information Technology can be used to develop new interactions between pupils, pupils and teacher and between pupils and knowledge. We also endeavour to explore the new opportunities IT offers for differentiating the approach used for individual learners, and for providing for greater continuity in the process of assessment.

Innovation in an educational system necessarily depends upon a large number of factors and involves all levels of the educational chain: central government authorities responsible for political choices and for introducing the measures to implement them, local authorities, school board members, advisers and head teachers, teachers in their individual classroom practice and parents who support or reject changes. Although I attempt to highlight the various factors at work in the projects observed, my objective is not to give a comparative overview of IT in European primary education systems, but rather to show the innovative ways in which class teachers have introduced IT in their daily classroom practice to develop in their pupils independent learning strategies. As the study proceeded, it became increasingly evident that one contributing factor to the success of IT integration is the time and effort spent by parents and volunteer workers to help with, or set up their own, IT projects; a full section has been dedicated to one such project.

Readers are now invited to embark upon a journey that relates the fabulous encounter of children, teachers and Information Technology through both the pedagogical analyses of on-site observations and the projections that I have attempted to make regarding the education of our children in the 21st century.

---

4. Council for Cultural Co-operation: School Education Division, *Innovation in Primary Education*, Strasbourg, Council of Europe, 1988, p.22
5. Council for Cultural Co-operation: School Education Division, *Innovation in Primary Education*, Strasbourg, Council of Europe, 1988, p. 7-12

SECTION ONE

A Tour of the Educational and Social Horizon

"It is wise to go there where progress leads us... humanity is blind."

NAPOLÉON

Chapter 1

Moving towards independent learning

Entering the Information Age

In 1753[1], when Tobias Mayer invented his famous Nautical Almanac based on the work of mathematician Leonhard Euler, the computer was already a twinkle in the eye of progress-driven humanity. His instrument remained the jealously guarded secret of the British Navy for close to a century, its precision sharply upgraded by the application of seven digit algorithms in 1834. In the 1880's, an enterprising American named Herman Hollerith saved the day in his local census bureau with his ingenious invention that used strategically placed holes in cards to record the statistics of the local population - he had inadvertently found an elementary support for codifying information in a binary code. And so the punch card system, forerunner to the computer, was born. Thomas Watson used this discovery to found IBM, his first business machines being based on the mechanical sequential reading of information. The second World War intensified inventive efforts on both sides of the Atlantic, culminating in the development of the ENIAC (Electronic Numerical Integrator and Computer) in 1945. From electronic valve-powered machines we progressed to transistors in the early fifties. Technological progress in the form of transistor radios then television brought media to the forefront in our daily lives. Then, in the early sixties, the first micro-chip was presented to the public. The veritable breakthrough in Information Technology came with the development of the disk, sequential access to information was replaced by indexed sequential and random access - real-time access to information was at last possible. The Information Age was well underway.

In the seventies, major institutions began using private lines to set up large network links for the transmission of data. By the eighties, the micro-chip had been sufficiently developed to allow the micro-computer to be linked to televisions screens and to networks via moderate-speed public servers. The personal computer got smaller and cheaper and was soon to become a household commodity. Rare were the economic sectors which did not fall under its pervasive influence over the ensuing decade. The information highway was already becoming jammed with private traffic, and the distance between nations

---

1. These first paragraphs are largely inspired by the works of Daniel Deberghes, Adminstrator of the Norbert Ségard Foundation and Senior Official, DG XIII (Telecommunication, Information and Innovation) of the European Commission

reduced to the seconds it took to transmit large masses of information across the planet. Through technological progress, the world was on its way to becoming what some consider a social, political and economic global village.

Basically, the computer can be compared to the machinery that heralded the approach of the Industrial Revolution. Information is the raw material on which it runs. The computer itself, once it has been programmed to receive data, can do no more than read, write, compare and calculate (compute). The way instructions are fed into it and the functions it carries out when the input has been processed depend on the type of input and output devices with which it is equipped. However, the multiplicity of its complex applications, the huge amount of numeric, alphabetic and symbolic data that can be almost instantaneously processed and the exponential rate of technological progress it has engendered have changed our lives forever.

These transformations brought in their wake a plethora of new demands on workers. Those who possess general but sufficiently broad qualifications have been able to take part in training programs to extend the domain and nature of their employment; those who have not benefited from a sound, broad-based elementary education adapt less easily. They are unable to learn the new and multiple skills needed to work with new technology, and soon forget their old skills as these fall into disuse[2]. The soaring figures of unemployment for older workers live on to tell the tale. Unfortunately, these transformations completely bypassed most teachers, who were given neither time off during working hours to attend training courses nor the opportunity to take part in a technological and sociological movement that was changing the pattern of the rest of our working lives.

The globalisation of economies has placed new demands on citizens, too. It is no longer sufficient to know what is going on in our immediate environment, to take an active role in the democracy of our nations citizens need a far greater awareness of the key issues in the field of politics, economics, social issues, history and culture. Most of these domains are undergoing constant change. In such a world, learning "how to learn" becomes as important as the content of learning. Without the capacity to embark on a journey of lifelong learning, individuals will find it difficult to master the increasingly complex situations encountered in both social and professional life, a factor which will eventually increase social tensions and contribute to the destruction of our social fabric[3].

The ultra-rapid communication modes developed throughout the 20th century have led to an extension of space and anonymity and an overwhelming complexity of the basic rules of life (the linear process of education-profession no longer applies). The individual is progressively losing his identity and

2. Haggis S., *L'Education pour tous: les objectifs et le contexte*, Monographie 1, Paris, UNESCO, 1993, p. 42 - 43

3. Cochinaux, P., de Woot, P., *Moving Towards a Learning Society*, Louvain, CRE-ERT, 1995, p.28-30

finding it increasingly difficult to navigate in the labyrinth of knowledge[4]. The traditional concept of socialisation through the inculcation and interiorisation of roles, norms and values no longer replies to the needs of the individual, perhaps because of the contradiction of our social institutions (family - schools - media - economic world), or perhaps because within each institution the proposed models are themselves contradictory. Today the individual must play an active role in building his own character and identity. He can "tinker" with his own identity by assembling various elements which are sometimes heterogeneous, or even contradictory, acquired through encounters at school or inside peer groups. He creates for himself a patchwork personality, becoming an actor in a "self-service" identity where everything is on display, but rather disordered. He has learnt to pick and choose according to his own needs and desires, which are conveyed by the cultural environment within the social and cultural milieu to which he belongs[5]. This holds vast implications for the education system if it is to fulfil its mission in preparing today's generation to become responsible citizens in our democracies.

With the mass of information instantly available in today's "Information Society" and the increasingly greater role played by the media in every facet of our daily lives, education can no longer confine itself to the microcosm of the school. It must train our future citizens for their lifelong road of learning by enabling them to develop the strategies necessary to sift through this mass of information for appropriateness, coherence, relevance, and even verity. In short, if we are to neutralise any demons that might escape from the Pandora's box that technological progress has opened, our educational systems need to become a reflection of the society they serve and teach children to use judiciously society's methods and tools.

Education in a rapidly changing world

The concept of school as we know it today is the vestige of a system hastily set up in the 19th century to greet the flood of learners brought to its doors in reply to the education bills which, in a number of European countries, rendered a basic knowledge of the three R's (reading, writing and arithmetic) compulsory. The cause of this public conscience crisis as regards to education was, of course, the Industrial revolution which transformed predominantly rural and agricultural countries into predominantly urban and manufacturing ones. The Industrial revolution brought into being a new class of skilled workers necessary to run the machines that were rapidly introduced to take over formerly manual tasks. History has shown the efficiency of 19th century national education systems - illiteracy was widespread at the turn of the century and today still represents a

---

4. Deberghes D., De la vie à l'école à l'école de la vie, in *Annales des Mines*, Paris, 1993, La Formation en Europe, p.59
5. Cochinaux, P., de Woot, P., *Moving Towards a Learning Society*, Louvain, CRE-ERT, 1995, p.28-30

handicap for an estimated 4% of western populations and a total of 900 million inhabitants on our planet.[6]

By the beginning of the 19th century primary education had, in most European nations, become compulsory for all children up to the age of 11 years. As economic and social conditions continued to evolve, the school progressively took on a much wider role than providing an elementary education in reading, writing and arithmetic, to become a vast public institution responsible for passing on social and cultural traditions. Its role in this domain is more important than ever in today's society with the gradual breakdown of family and social structures. Little else has changed in the world of education though the world around is being transformed at a stupendous rate. Indeed, what can change as long as chalk and blackboard remain the most widespread teaching aid, teachers are confronted with class numbers that make individualised teaching almost impossible, the national curriculum dictates the content of lessons taking into no account children's interests or the concept of associations between subject areas, and assessment methods continue to rate the individual's achievement in terms of class average instead of being used as a yardstick to measure the distance covered by each in the long and arduous road to becoming an independent learner? And little will change until teachers are given access to the new information tools that are changing the world, the very tools that are changing the needs of learners who, for the most part, will require

"The world of education according to Daumier"

6. Delors J., *L'Education: un trésor est caché dedans*, Paris, UNESCO/Editions Odile Jacob, 1996, p. 21

"The world of education according to Daumier"

computer-literacy and basic skills and strategies in information handling as a prerequisite to almost any employment sector they may choose for their professional career.

The education system has become one of the major social institutions of our modern society. As with all vast institutions, evolution is a slow process, and rightfully so given the enormous responsibility that it has been entrusted as guardian of our culture and traditions and training ground for all future citizens of our democracy. However, change is also being bridled by a number of other factors that we shall now examine more closely.

The national education systems of the fifteen member states in the European Union today employ a total of more than four million teachers and cater to the needs of some 26 million pupils at primary and secondary levels,[7] hence making education the largest single "employment" sector in all nations. These figures become more meaningful when we consider the graph below, which shows the percentage of pupils and teacher in the population in each of the European Union nations.

FIGURE 1

TEACHERS & PUPILS PER TOTAL POPULATION IN EUROPEAN NATIONS
Year 1992/1993 (primary and secondary school levels only)

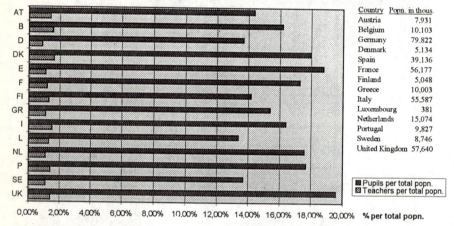

Country	Popn. in thous.
Austria	7,931
Belgium	10,103
Germany	79,822
Denmark	5,134
Spain	39,136
France	56,177
Finland	5,048
Greece	10,003
Italy	55,587
Luxembourg	381
Netherlands	15,074
Portugal	9,827
Sweden	8,746
United Kingdom	57,640

Source: EUROSTAT

If we break down this information further, to examine the pupil/teacher ratio at the primary education level, we begin to realise the Herculean task facing teachers who are conscious of the need to individualise their teaching and wish to cater to the different learning rhythms and aptitudes of their pupils (Fig. 2, see p. 25).

This graph shows the mean average per country and is therefore not truly indicative of the reality of the situation, since many schools in geographically isolated regions have far less pupils than those in more populated areas. The average number of pupils in the classes observed throughout this study ranged from 20 - 30, except in Luxembourg where the figure was considerably lower (15 - 17). A teacher trainer encountered at the University of Münster, Rhineland Westphalia, indicates that the pupil/teacher ratio is generally much higher in

---

7. Eurydice, *Key data on Education in the EU - 1995, European Commission (Education, Training and Youth,* Brussels, European Commission, 1996, p. 96. (Figures not available for Ireland).

FIGURE 2

AVERAGE NUMBER OF PUPILS PER TEACHER IN EUROPEAN PRIMARY SCHOOLS
Year 1992/1993 (both public and private sectors included)

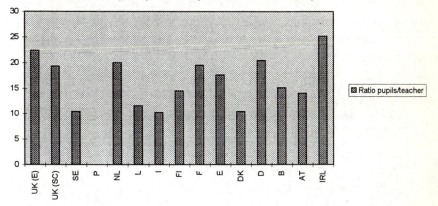

Source: Eurydice. From the publication "Key data on education in the EU - 1995. European Commission (Education, Training and Youth)".

Germany. Italy has adopted a unique system, developed as a consequence of the sharp drop in birth rates over the past decade, whereby in certain areas two teachers are appointed per class. In other areas, three teachers share the responsibility of two classes.

Although, partly due to a general decrease in birth rates, the number of pupils per class has been appreciably reduced in most regions in Europe over the past few years, the reverse side of the coin is that the annual intake of trainee teachers in universities and training institutions has also decreased. The age pyramid amongst the teaching population is currently very top heavy. The percentage of teachers over the age of 50 range from 11% (Austria) to 36% (Sweden) whereas, at the other end of the scale, teachers under the age of 30 account for just 4% of the primary school teaching population in Denmark to slightly over 20% in Belgium, Ireland and Austria. This factor definitely contributes to the slow integration of new pedagogical approaches in general and of Information Technology in particular, especially since practising teachers are given little incentive to update their methods through in-service training and, even if they were encouraged to do so, rare are the in-service courses on offer in the domain of Information Technology. Most of the IT-using teachers encountered in this study were aged between 30 and 40. Younger teachers, particularly those fortunate enough to have discovered the value of IT in their own learning experiences, are probably also high IT-users in the classroom but head teachers are often reluctant to use "inexperienced teachers" as an example of the work being carried out in their schools.

Bridging the gap between family and society

With the gradual weakening of family structures over the past half-century brought about to a large extent by the pressures of modern life and woman's role in the professional arena, ever increasing responsibilities are being cast onto the elementary education system. Ideally, the school has six primary and fundamental functions[8]:

- **to teach:** the transmission of knowledge (facts, methods, key concepts) and skills, not only the three R's but also the skills of communication, deduction, prediction, formulation of hypotheses, seeking of relationships and decision-making that will enable citizens to survive in a rapidly changing world. A willingness to hypothesise and interrogate hypotheses are essential cognitive tools, both in the basic skill of reading and in conceptual development generally.[9] Although vitally important, the transmission of knowledge in itself is not enough. Above and beyond knowledge, it is important to develop a know-how-to-do and -be. The object of learning is to learn how to learn and think, rather than merely accumulate facts.

- **to instil the values of society:** but how can the school maintain its traditional role in handing down the values of society when the very values of society are being called into question? If it cannot, who is ready to take on this role?

- **to socialise:** this is an increasingly important function in view of the diminished role assumed by families today. Children are socialised through their encounters with other children at school. School is in itself a mini-society which not only provides many children with their first experience in horizontal relationships, it also represents for many their first encounter with authority and discipline; it is at school that children begin to modify their behaviour in response to aggressivity and all the other elements that constitute life in a group. They learn to communicate (speaking, listening, negotiating), work in teams, cope with group dynamics, accept people as individuals and develop an awareness of the values of society.

- **pre-professionalisation**, although in most cases the gap between school and the working world prevents schools from fulfilling this role. Since the rhythm of technological developments often renders training obsolete, it is more important to teach children how to live and develop the interdisciplinary approach they will need to deal with the different types of work now required by professional life.

- **unification of the social corps** - "democracy through education". It is the school's responsibility to promote equality of independent learning capacity and thereby enable each individual to exploit his full learning potential. Alas, as yet school has not succeeded in making up for the difficulties of

8. Ségard N. (Minister of Telecommunications), *Technologies et Société: Rapport au Premier Ministre*, Paris, La Documentation Française, 1985, p. 70-71
9. Cox M., Johnson D.C., *The ImpacT Report*, London, King's College, 1993, p.76

certain children handicapped by insufficient or inappropriate learning experiences in their early years.

- **providing supervision** throughout the day. Here, the role of the school is
being continually extended in response to weakening family structures.
Today even 16 and 18 year-olds seek the protective "hearth" the school has
to offer.

Primary school, the first and most vital link in the educational chain setting
the pattern for all subsequent learning experiences, has the major responsibility
of carrying out most of these functions. It is for this reason that, in 1988, the
Council of Europe[10] redefined the goals of primary education and went so far as
to suggest that an explicit Common Charter be drawn up between member
countries to clearly outline the mission of primary education in light of recent
educational research. The findings of a survey carried out on innovation in
primary school by its School Education Division, and relevant statements made
by its Committee of Ministers in a declaration on "Intolerance, a threat to
democracy" (14 May, 1981), reveal that primary education in our modern
society should:

- extend beyond the basic skills of reading, writing and arithmetic, even
though these are still important;

- give children a wider perception of their immediate and distant cultural and
physical environment;

- stimulate children's general development according to their full physical
and intellectual potential, foster their aesthetic awareness and provide them with
opportunities for artistic expression and creativity;

- enable children to acquire and exercise the democratic values of
participation, responsibility, respect for the rights and opinions of others, and the
development of understanding and solidarity;

- take into account the personal and cultural characteristics of each child and
seek to develop his or her personality, with special attention to moral, social and
ethical questions;

- stimulate the development of values, interests, knowledge, ideas, life skills,
know-how and learning techniques and attitudes, thus preparing children for the
demands of secondary education, work, the family and the community.

Investing in the future

But are we providing our education systems the means to carry out these
goals? Barber Conable, President of the World Bank, declared at the opening of
the UNESCO world conference on "Education for All" (Thailand) in March

---

10. Council for Cultural Co-operation: School Education Division, *Innovation in Primary Education*, Strasbourg, Council of Europe, 1988, p.7-22.

1990: "Money spent on education is a sound investment. This can be seen both on the level of national budgets and private income. When citizens are educated, their income rises, as does savings, investment and, in the long term, the well-being of the whole society." Few citizens would doubt the verity of his statement yet, despite being the sector catering to the direct needs of well over 16% of the entire European population (pre-school and post-secondary institutions are not included in the data given in Figure 1) and the indirect needs of society as a whole, the overall budget allocated to education in 1990/1991 ranged from 404 ECU per inhabitant in Portugal* to 878 ECU per inhabitant in France (figures from Greece, Italy and Luxembourg were not available).[11] Most of this money is spent on meeting the day-to-day needs of educational institutions (Figure 3), very little on renewing educational material and equipping schools with the tools so vital to them if they are to face the challenges that lie ahead. How many public or private institutions could survive in this day and age with such a limited budget attributed to investment?

FIGURE 3

BREAKDOWN OF NATIONAL EXPENDITURE ON EDUCATION IN 1992/1993

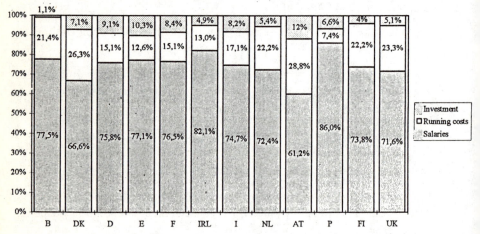

Source : Eurydice. From the publication "Key data on education in the EU - 1995. European Commission (Education, Training and Youth)".

Now that we have briefly examined some of the key issues that are jeopardising the capacities of educational institutions to carry out the tasks attributed to them by our nations, let us move on to the challenges confronting future generations of learners if they are to succeed in taking their rightful place in society tomorrow.

---

* In countries such as Portugal, with a low contribution per inhabitant, certain educational actions are financed by the Structural Funds of the European Commission.

11. Eurydice, *Key data on education in the EU - 1994*, Brussels, European Commission: Education, Training and Youth, 1995, p. 56.

Towards a learning society

If schools are to fulfil the mission attributed to them by society, then they must keep up with the pace of society, introducing into the classroom and the learning process the tools with which tomorrow's citizen will work. They must also satisfy and discipline the appetite the media has whet by providing pupils with an opportunity to critically explore the world in image, sound and colour. However, even this is not enough. The Information Society so highly praised by the EU Delors White Paper must be completed and matched by a Learning Society, if we do not want to fall into an over-informed world and a valueless culture based on "zapping" and "patchwork" superficiality.

Sir C. Ball, member of the Royal Society for the Encouragement of Arts, Manufactures and Commerce, describes the Learning Society as one in which[12]:

- learning is accepted as a continuing activity throughout life
- learners take responsibility for their own progress
- assessment confirms progress rather than brands failure
- capability, personal and shared values and team work are recognised as much as the pursuit of knowledge
- learning is a partnership between students, parents, teachers, employers and the community, who all work together to improve performance[13].

The educational system of the future must become more open, offer more alternatives and fewer hierarchical restraints. Knowledge itself is becoming less hierarchical and today's data support systems (disks, CD-ROMs, Internet, data banks, etc.) provide an ideal opportunity to move the emphasis from "learning by heart" to association-connection network-type strategies. These call on long-term rather than short-term memory in the learning process[14] and can be used by the learner for the rest of his life. The teacher is no longer "the custodian of knowledge", his ability depends not on knowledge but on the professional skills brought to bear on the learning needs of pupils and his capacity to motivate them in their lifelong journey of exploration and enquiry.

By the turn of the 21st century, an elementary knowledge of information technology will be necessary for all types of employment, from industrial to service sectors. Basic scientific and technical culture in information technology will constitute an indispensable means of developing competitive edge in economic sectors and providing citizens with a new mode of communication throughout their lives.

Europe[15], and more recently the European Union, has always worked towards fulfilling the aspirations of the population in the aim of developing a

12. *RSA Journal*, May 1992, p.384
13. Cochinaux, P., de Woot, P., *Moving Towards a Learning Society*, Louvain, CRE-ERT, 1995, p.52
14. de Landsheere, V., *L'education et la formation*, Paris, PUF, 1992, p.55-57
15. Deberghes D., La Formation en Europe in *Annales des Mines*, Paris, 1993,

true democracy in which each citizen is able to assume his own responsibility. The three key issues have always been:

- to provide each citizen with adequate means of communication and points of reference - reading, writing and arithmetic (the 3 R's in the 19th century)
- to assist in the redeployment of the working world towards new types of employment (1960)
- to consider in-service training as a strategic investment (1970).

Today the European Union is confronted with a new political reality: if citizens are to cope with the increasingly complex relationships now developing between the individual and the community, they must learn to master a fourth mode of communication - electronic information resources. Our citizens need to learn how to choose from the mass of information available (navigate) and create their own cognitive networks through individual assimilation of the reasoning process. Only in this way can they retain optimum control over the decision-making process.

Initial training can no longer produce a "finished product" or supply an adequate "stock of knowledge" for the rest of our lives, but rather it should aim at preparing the ground for lifelong learning by encouraging an arborescent-type logic through the development of inductive and deductive reasoning strategies. If this new requirement is not taken into account at the European Union level, "electronic information will become an unsurmountable problem leading to the irremediable disruption of the social order," (according to a statement made by D. Deberghes, of the Norbert Ségard Foundation in France)[16].

The present study was conceived as an attempt to record (by use of the standard observation grids included in this publication) some of the innovative projects that are currently underway in Europe. Through the use of IT, learning in the primary school can be promoted from level 1 (to learn) to level 2 (provide a meaningful learning environment that the pupil can carry with him throughout his life). We also endeavour to assess the changes IT brings, not only in pupil-teacher relationships, but also in social interactions between pupils and pupils' attitudes in regards to knowledge. The analyses drawn from these observations aim at highlighting the underlying reasons for the resounding success of certain projects, but also at determining the areas in which greater effort is called for. The findings of the study were submitted to the European Union in June 1996 with the list of recommendations outlined in the conclusion in the hope that measures can be taken at a European level.

---

16. Deberghes D., *La Formation aux Technologies de l'Information et de la Communication en Europe et la Subsidiarité* (AFCET International Congress, Versailles, 1993)

Deberghes D., *L'information électronique, vecteur de croissance ou de crise, de la révolution Gutenberg à la révolution Shannon*, Luxembourg, C.C.E. XIII, 1993

Chapter 2

Enhancing the learning process

Information Technology as a learning tool

Since the turn of the 19th century, educational theorists and psychologists have been lobbying for major reforms in the educational system, in an effort to renew the alliance that should exist between school and society. As early as 1916, John Dewey urged educationalists to relate education to students' interests, stressing the need for pupils to have instruments and tools favouring group activity and co-operation, and insisting that a greater number of interactions and learning possibilities could free the child from the influence of verbalisation and authoritative explanations of teachers and adults. "The idea of education set forth in these chapters is the idea of continuous reconstruction of experience"[17]. He advocated a student-centred rather than subject-centred school, education through activity rather than formal learning, and vocational or occupational education rather than mastery of traditional subjects. A second basis of educational reform, as Dewey saw it, required an analysis of contemporary society, its aims and needs. He was referring to the changes wrought by the Industrial Revolution, but his words seem particularly pertinent today. Not only does IT provide one of the learning tools to which he referred, it is also directly related to the aims and needs of the 20th century Information Society.

In fact, as Seymour Papert pointed out in one of his recent works: "With much more persuasive power than the philosophy of even so radical a thinker as Dewey, the computer, in all its various manifestations, is offering the Yearners (those yearning for reform in the educational system) new opportunities to craft alternatives. The only question that remains is, Will such alternatives be created democratically? Will public education systems lead the way or, as in most things, will the change first enhance the lives of the children of the wealthy and powerful and only slowly and with much effort find its way into the lives of the children of the rest of us? Will School continue to impose a single type of knowing on everyone, or will it adapt to an epistemological pluralism?"[18].

17. Dewey J., *Democracy and Education*, New York, The Macmillan Company, 1916, p.93
18. Papert S., *The Children's Machine: Rethinking School in the Age of the Computer*, New York, Harvester/Wheatsheaf, 1993, p.6

Although we should be a little wary of using the term "persuasive power" in reference to the computer, the mass of immediately accessible information it makes available is having an undeniable influence on both the collective and individual mode of thought. This is certainly a delicate issue that must be taken into consideration at the primary school level if our children are to acquire a sufficient degree of discernment as they gradually develop the processes of inductive and deductive reasoning.

Papert's interrogations ring a bell of warning when we consider that 10% of European households own a computer. Who owns these computers? The figures on computer ownership presented in the "Children of the Future" project on page 96 suggest that their distribution is all but democratic. Are we to sit by as passive spectators and watch the cleavage deepen in what some already call a two-tier society? Or are we to seize this opportunity to equalise the chances of pupils from less-privileged socio-economic environments? IT-competent teachers are unanimous in their conclusion that children with learning difficulties - be it through lack of motivation, concentration or self-confidence, poor language skills or learning impairments - reap the greatest benefit from using computers in class. In this respect it is satisfying to learn from educational authorities in France, Portugal, Italy and England that a great number of communities in under-privileged areas are making tremendous efforts to raise funds for the purchase of information technology equipment for their local schools - as if they realise that at last they have an opportunity to make up for the injustices of nature (and society).

Assessing the value of IT in the learning process

And so slowly the computer is making its way into the primary classroom, although I am not sure that in many schools the continuous reconstruction of experience that Dewey dreamed of can become a reality. Little research has been carried out on the subject; it seems that Research and Development is a concept that has not yet earned itself a place in the realm of education. The OECD, UNESCO and the Council of Europe have drawn up a number of international reports stressing the need for Information Technology at all education levels. The IEA (International Association for the Evaluation of Educational Achievement) carried out a study in 1993 in 21 nations to examine the degree of innovation in their educational systems, but to my knowledge few studies have been made to examine the effects of this new medium integrated into a global learning process at the middle primary school level.

One publication which served as an invaluable basis in the present study is the ImpacT Report[19]. Drawn up from an assessment made in England and Wales on the intrinsic value of Information Technology on pupils' learning and

---

19. This section is almost entirely based upon ideas expressed by Cox M.J., Johnson D.C., The ImpacT Report, London, King's College, 1993, in particular on p.1 and p.156

classroom activity in the core subject areas of mathematics, science, geography and English, it was the first large scale comprehensive, longitudinal and in-depth investigation undertaken in any country or region. Focusing on the potential impact of IT on pupils' achievements across a broad age band and a range of school subjects, the findings of this report leave little room for doubt - IT enhances the learning environment in numerous ways. Sufficient data is as yet unavailable to determine whether the learning gains induced by this new learning medium will have a long-term effect on the learning potential of pupils, but some of the immediate learning gains arising from IT use in the classroom are reported as follows:

- computers are found to be good motivation, heightening pupils' interest and enjoyment of subjects - motivation is intricately linked with increased concentration and sustained effort;
- heightened interest and enjoyment have a positive effect upon the status of the subject in which IT is used;.
- computers aid concentration by focusing pupils' attention on the work at hand and, as a result, some pupils and teachers believe that the standard of work produced is of a higher quality than it would have been otherwise;
- involvement in IT-incorporated activities is often sustained over quite lengthy periods - sometimes an hour or more - regardless of the pupil's age;
- IT provides new opportunities to work in an open-ended way, enabling pupils to become involved in more complex and challenging learning situations beyond those typically experienced;
- where pupils use software to improve the presentation of their work, they often show more pride in their product, as contrasted with that achieved with more conventional media;
- some pupils are keen to continue with IT work outside normal lesson time and continue to discuss activities after the lesson is over - they appear to retain knowledge of what they have experienced over time;
- conceptual misunderstandings are often made more apparent through the interaction with a computing environment, since IT provides for a greater understanding of detail and "connectedness".

Observations made during the present study consolidate the findings of the ImpacT Report and, in fact, lead me to believe that a sufficient number of computers in the classroom - one computer for three or four children appears to be an ideal target - can fundamentally alter organisational methods in such a way that we should no longer simply speak of learning gains, but rather of an enhanced learning environment that actively involves children. This creates a socialisation process that could have far reaching effects on adaptation in the social, and eventually professional, world.

The Ampère Study - objectives and methodology

The objectives of the present study are somewhat different from those of the ImpacT Report. Instead of focusing our sights on learning gains in specific subject areas, we were seeking evidence that, when used in a global approach to learning, Information Technology can induce new learning methods, i.e. the pupil no longer accumulates knowledge in a teacher-directed environment but is encouraged to develop the skills and strategies which will lead him to become an independent lifelong learner, ready to face the complex situations he encounters in life. A second objective of the study was to measure the ways in which Information Technology could be used to promote equality of independent learning capacity and enable each individual to realise his full learning potential. Three major obstacles are at present preventing a great number of our citizens from realising their full learning capacities and hence taking their rightful place in the democracy of our nations:

- learning difficulties due, not only to learning impairments, but also to the socio-economic environment in which children are brought up,
- the inability to carry out formal operational reasoning, a form of reasoning inherent to the decision-making process,
- physical handicaps which prevent certain children from developing autonomy in learning and from taking part in mainstream education, hence limiting their possibilities to socialise with physically able children of their own age.

The question is: What can Information Technology bring to the learning process to help overcome these obstacles?

In view of the changing demands on citizens in our information rich society, the Ampère study also set out to analyse how use of IT with middle-primary school children can:

- promote skills of deduction, prediction, seeking of relationships, independent formulation and verification of hypotheses,
- develop creativity, interdisciplinarity and communication skills,
- produce positive interactions and new and rewarding dimensions in teacher to pupil, pupil to pupil, pupil to knowledge and pupil to outside world relationships that will enrich the learning environment.

Of course, Information Technology - equipment, software and methods for automatic processing and transmission of information and the associated know-how[20] - is no more than a learning medium, its capacities limited to the four basic functions mentioned in Chapter I. All of the above objectives are entirely dependent upon the way the teacher incorporates IT into his teaching program.

---

20. Finnish Ministry of Education, *Education, Training and Research in the Information Society: A National Strategy*, Helsinki, Ministry of Education, 1995, p. 76

An underlying objective was therefore to assess the role of the teacher in a learning environment where children are encouraged to direct their own learning activities. IT-incorporated activities necessarily change organisational methods in teaching, since they place a greater emphasis on pair and group work; teachers must succeed in encouraging pupils to work in a motivated and self-directed manner if they are to carry out their tasks efficiently without constant supervision. Secondly, if children are to gain maximum benefit from learning activities organised around peer interactions, groups must be carefully constituted, taking into account the personality and ability of each. Individualisation takes on a far greater importance - the teacher must keep his finger on the learning pulse of every member of his class; sense when his intervention is necessary and know how to choose projects that correspond both to the interests and the learning goals of his pupils. These goals can only be set through close collaboration between teacher and pupil, and by the introduction of assessment methods that follow individual progress and assist learners in settings their own goals.

Our long-term objectives, defined in collaboration with the European Commission, were to identify the factors conducive to effective use of IT in the classroom then trace their origin and suggest means for their reproduction on a wider scale, in particular by identifying teacher needs. We were also continually on the lookout for any negative effects that IT may have on the learning process; these are discussed in Chapter 7.

Once the objectives had been drawn up, the second step was to design an observation grid (presented alongside the relevant projects in the following chapters) that could be used by teachers themselves to analyse the process taking place in their classrooms. A second "Background" grid, included in the Annex, was drawn up to give readers information they may find useful in terms of project funding and assessment, teacher training, organisational methods, further reading and contact addresses. The next step was the most difficult. If the education system can be considered as the stronghold of the culture and tradition of a nation, then gaining access to classrooms can, in many cases, be compared to gaining entrance to a holy inner sanctum. Although educational authorities are usually quite eager to talk about work being carried out on pilot sites, they are often less enthusiastic about having outsiders sit in for half a day in one of their classrooms. On the whole, once their confidence had been gained (this takes time and travel, and explains why not all of the 15 European member states were included in the study) and suitable projects chosen, they were most supportive in their actions. It must be mentioned that, in many countries, responsibility for supervising the integration of IT in primary schools is left to a very small committee, often composed of ex-teaching staff, who first had to be granted permission from their hierarchy before allowing access to classrooms.

In countries for which language or distance represented too great a problem, teachers themselves carried out the observations.

A further difficulty that often hampered the progress of this study, but a factor that is considerably enriching the process of IT integration, is that innovation has become to a large extent a "bottom-up" action initiated by teachers, teacher associations, hardware and software distributors, parents and volunteer workers. Such projects often escape the watchful eye of the department of education and are known only to those directly concerned.

Despite these obstacles, however, a sufficient number of observations were made to prove that, in all corners of Europe, Information Technology is far more than simply a tool in the learning environment, but can be considered a catalyst that could radically change the face of education forever.

Preliminary findings

In his recent publication *L'Education: un trésor est caché dedans*, Mr Jacques Delors suggests that education can only fulfil its broader mission if it is organised around four basic types of learning which should become four fundamental pillars of knowledge: learning to know, learning to do, learning to live together, learning to be. I shall, for the length of this section, borrow the terms coined by Mr Delors as they seem to sum up perfectly the contributions that emerged throughout this study as being directly related to the effective use of IT in the classroom.

Learning to know - change is currently taking place at such a rate that an estimated 15 - 20% of the existing knowledge base in many sectors will become obsolete every year. Some estimates claim that two thirds of the technology needed by the year 2000 has yet to be invented[21]. Under such conditions it serves little purpose to fill a child's head with knowledge that will very likely become obsolete before he has a chance to use it in his professional life. In classes using computers, problem-solving, exploration of resources and autonomy in learning become the key issues. Children are invited to discover and master their own knowledge-seeking skills that will serve them for the rest of their lives. Problem-solving strategies are inherent to the process; the learner cannot embark on the process of collecting, sorting, organising and applying knowledge until he has drawn up hypotheses on possible solutions to the task in hand. Through trial and error, pupils perfect their ability to ask precise questions and come to understand the necessity of clearly defining research parameters before beginning a task. Not only do they learn to navigate in a mass of information in order to extract the knowledge needed - contrary to popular belief, books too have an important place in IT-equipped classrooms -, they also

21. European Commission, Lifelong Learning, in issue 4 of *Le Magazine for Education, Training and Youth in Europe*, Brussels, European Commission, 1995, p. 4.

*"Do not worry about your difficulties in mathematics ;
I can assure you that mine are still greater."*

Albert EINSTEIN

Computer-produced image (1975)

develop a greater facility for finding the most appropriate source of information and learn to use their sense of judgement in assessing the value of information obtained. By giving children a greater degree of autonomy in applying basic skills and strategies in their learning, knowledge becomes far more than what the teacher says or what they read in a book; the ready-made formulae learnt at school become part of a dynamic process that links school to the outside world, allowing the learner to understand underlying concepts and know how and when to apply them.

Information technology places far more emphasis on literacy, not just literacy in the traditional sense of the word (though this is vital if users are to decipher operating manuals and follow plans and schema), but also a high level of literacy in mathematics, science and technology. At the same time, computers essentially communicate by text, therefore providing an inherent incentive for children to improve their skills of reading and writing.

Learning to do is closely linked to learning to know. The challenge facing education today is to find methods that will succeed in transforming school knowledge into practical competence. It is now generally accepted that the most efficient and pertinent teaching is that which leads learners to solve the problems that they encounter in life and that are immediately attached to life, rather than learning by rote or repetitive exercises. There is a fundamental need to incorporate "doing" in learning, otherwise learning cannot have its natural outcome in action.[22]

The computer multiplies the teacher's capacity to involve his and her pupils in a "learning by doing" process. With a sufficient number of computers in class, each group of pupils can have its own "tool" permitting it to carry out its own experiments rather than having one group "doing", the rest of the class watching. A wide range of software exists today that caters to "learning by doing", hence enabling pupils to become physically involved in the learning process, to develop greater confidence in their own capacities and to develop a greater sense of autonomy at an early age. Several observations recorded in the following chapters highlight the enormous step forward that has been made through the use of IT in providing for even severely handicapped learners to learn by doing, thereby extending their autonomy in ways that could not have been imagined a decade ago.

Learning to live together is the only possible means of overcoming the exclusion, oppression and war that is wreaking havoc on society today. The social, economic and political globalisation of the world that is underway at present places a far greater responsibility on the shoulders of citizens, not always capable of understanding that their own actions will inevitably have far

---

22. Haggis S., *L'Education pour tous: les objectifs et le contexte, Monographie I*, Paris, UNESCO, 1993, P. 42-43.

reaching effects on those around them. At the classroom level, IT brings greater opportunities for children to work together, to develop a sense of team spirit, to appreciate the value of individual effort for the good of all. The authoritarian model still existing in many classrooms inculcates the opposite of this objective.

How can citizens learn to work together in society if they do not master the art at school? Information Technology-incorporated lessons engender new organisational methods favouring group interactions through the sharing of learning tools, and by encouraging a more collaborative, co-operative teacher-pupil relationship. They work together and learn from each other - children are often more competent in using computers than their teachers. Electronic network projects go one step further by breaking down national boundaries. Groups of learners in different countries are now working together via the information highway, thereby creating a global community of pupils who naturally come to appreciate the value of other cultural and ethnic groups in an electronic world blind to colour and creed.

Learning to live together also implies that each citizen develop sufficient reasoning capacities to make decisions as a responsible member of the community. True democracy can only exist if every individual is given the opportunity to develop his full reasoning potential, which he can only do if he is given the learning "space" to test his own theories and concepts and so advance in the spiral of cognitive development. Living together in harmony depends on every individual being able to exercise his own sense of judgement, without this he will remain at the mercy of the media, sensationalism and the new dangers of loss of privacy and individual freedom that the information age has accentuated.

Learning to be - in traditional classrooms children are given little occasion to express themselves, or even to be themselves. The golden rule is "speak when spoken to" (by the teacher), the goal is to cover the prescribed curriculum, the assessment methods compare individual results against a class average. Every learner has a learning rhythm and aptitudes of his own. Until schools succeed in individualising teaching methods to suit learners' needs and promote assessment methods that take learning differences into account, few pupils can *learn to be* at school. By extending the teacher's possibilities to provide individualised work for each pupil, the computer is already bringing about radical changes in this domain. Greater emphasis on group work is another step in the right direction. Children have a marvellous capacity for recognising the qualities of their fellow pupils; it is amusing to listen to the distribution of tasks around the computer. "You can type, you're faster", "You can draw the pictures that we're going to scan, you're good at drawing"... Surprisingly enough, the result is not that the same children do the same tasks at every project session, but rather that, by developing self-confidence in what they are good at, children gain incentive to try out new roles and to discover the full dimensions of their own identity.

The far-reaching effects that Information Technology is having on the learning environment are mirrored in the changing role of IT-using teachers. Gradually they are shedding the former "school master" approach to take on the guise of a "coach" spurring on each member of the team to make greater efforts, whilst sitting on the sidelines and letting the child get on with his own learning process. Of course, this is a Utopian vision inspired by visits to a handful of classrooms in which IT has been successfully integrated into daily teaching practice. Current figures on the integration of Information Technology in primary education in Europe are somewhat less optimistic.

IT integration progress to date

The ImpacT Report suggests that there is a minimum threshold of access for the contribution of IT to pupils' learning. If this is so, overall findings from the present study indicate that this minimum threshold is only rarely being reached. Although all figures on the integration of IT in primary education in European member states are not yet available, it seems that few schools can offer their pupils more than spasmodic IT access. In England, where an intensive effort on behalf of both the government and private sectors* has been made to equip schools, the ratio stands at 18:1 (30:1 in 7% of schools); in the Netherlands the Comenius-PRINT project has succeeded in equipping over 99% of primary and special schools with a ratio of 110:1 in the smallest schools (not including special schools where the ratio is 110:8) and 60:1 in the largest primary schools. In other countries such as Luxembourg, Italy and Portugal, computers are provided by local municipalities and therefore no state-wide ratio can be provided. It is interesting to note that a number of private schools renown for their progressive approach and their "active learning" philosophy (e.g. "free schools" in the Netherlands) are reluctant to include IT in their curriculum on the grounds that it will create a new barrier between the pupil and his natural environment.

Although most of the national curriculum today make specific mention of the use of IT even in the earliest grades, in most cases a global learning approach is still a concept unheard of or unheeded by the educational hierarchy. Subject are sliced up into a set number of "learning hours" with little attention given to the value of associations between subjects as a means of creating a more meaningful learning environment. Work programs are still set for each school grade, listing the operations that should be covered if the child is to progress to the next class. G. Delacôte[23] suggests following the example slowly being introduced in the United States, whereby work programs are replaced by subject standards defined for a four year period and serving as instruments that

---

* *A supermarket chain in England has created a token-scheme. Customers hand in their tokens to their local school which, when it has collected the required amount, receives a free computer (corresponding to the norms of the National Department of Education).*

23. Delacôte G., *Savoir apprendre les nouvelles méthodes*, Paris, Editions Odile Jacob, 1996, p. 223

will help teachers choose both the contents of their program and the most judicious methods of implementing it, in keeping with the situation specific to each class. A method along these lines has now been introduced in England, where the curriculum has broken away from the tradition of vertical organisation in "grades" and is now horizontally organised into Key Stages (KS) - KS1 usually includes 4-7 year-olds, KS 2 basically refers to 7-11 year olds. Each child continues to work through a Key Stage until he has reached the required attainment level. Attainment levels comprise a set of ideas, principles, knowledge and skills that the child can master at his own rhythm in a spiral progression[24]. This method of progression overcomes the negative social effects of "staying back" but also underlines the needs for a new approach to assessment, as pupils can no longer be assessed on a class level, but must be assessed individually in reference to their own aptitudes and learning rhythm.

Despite lack of school-provided equipment and the constraints of curriculum, class inspectors and such, an appreciable number of teachers in Europe and throughout the world are already enthusiastically working in the intimacy of their classroom to introduce this new medium in an effort to enhance their teaching/learning environment and help pupils to develop their full potential as independent lifelong learners. Because of the lack of training facilities available to them, a large percentage of these have acquired their computer literacy through a personal interest in Information Technology, contacts with friends and family, or professional needs to produce teaching aids or cope with the heavy administrative tasks expected of them. Others have come to discover the intrinsic potential of IT through their contact with children and their interest in how their pupils spend their time out of school hours. In some instances, teachers use their own hardware and software in class, or take it upon themselves to approach the municipality, parents or manufacturers to compensate for the lack of resources provided by their hierarchy.

Change is slow in the world of education, but how much longer can we ignore the fact that a new alliance must be formed between education and society?

---

24. de Landsheere V., *L'Education et la Formation*, France, PUF, 1992, p.406-411

SECTION TWO

Applying IT in European Primary Education

"A good teacher has but one concern:
succeed in teaching his pupils to live without him."

André GIDE

The way the computer is used in the teaching/learning process naturally depends on the amount and type of material available. When a teacher has access to just one computer, this is more often than not used as a teaching (but not learning) aid, somewhat like a blackboard in motion; the teacher inputs the data, or chooses one of his pupils to work at the keyboard, other pupils passively watch the screen display (with difficulty considering the size of the screen and the quality of the image) but no real pupil/computer interaction can take place. Admittedly the pupils are being treated to a new classroom experience, but one cannot help but ask the question: "Above and beyond the motivation factor inherent to the use of any novel teaching aid, what learning gains can we realistically expect to achieve?". Some more enterprising teachers divide the class into groups and send one group at a time to work on the computer whilst the rest of the class work on complementary or preparation activities. Once again we must ask the question: "With such limited access what sustainable learning gains can be achieved?" This type of activity necessitates extra time and effort on behalf of the teacher in terms of class organisation, work preparation, supervision, technical trouble-shooting, and correction of work. Under these circumstances, we can understand the reticence of most teachers bemoaning lack of time, lack of training, lack of computer experience, lack of material, etc., as excuses to avoid the issue of introducing IT into classroom practice.

But rare are the primary school classes in Europe that are even fortunate enough to have access to even one computer all day long. In many cases, the computer is set up on a moveable trolley and computer access is painstakingly programmed a week, a month or a term in advance in order to give every child the smallest degree of access. In other cases, the computers are set up in a laboratory or in the school resource centre and the class must move out of the everyday classroom context, with all the material disadvantages and the disruption that this entails, if they are to benefit from their computer time slot - rarely consisting of any more than one hour per week.

Besides the lack of hardware in primary classes, a third criteria which plays a determining role in the way IT is being applied is the availability of software. In this respect, most teachers can do no more than to comply with the selections made by the school board, head teachers or voted by the teaching staff majority.

Taking into account these factors, I have included in this section not only descriptions of projects underway, but also potential applications highlighted in earlier reports on the subject or underlined by the teachers and educational authorities encountered during this study. Some of the classroom observations to follow were carried out by teachers, IT co-ordinators or project-leaders.

It seems from our findings that applications of Information Technology in primary education basically fall into five categories:

• *Computer Assisted Instruction (CAI) and drills*

• *Control technology*

(these two require task-specific software)

• *Expression and communication*

• *Data-logging and information handling*

(for these applications, general-purpose software can be used)

• *Reference resources*

(using wider application, read-only software or the information highway).

For each of these categories, I have included a description of learning gains that have been noted as a direct result of effective IT usage, as well as a discussion on new paths to learning they could engender. The observation grids used to record our findings are presented with the respective projects. The "Background" grid can be found in the Annex.

Chapter 3

Using task-oriented software

Computer Assisted Instruction and drills

CAI (Computer Assisted Instruction) and drills were reported by the IEA (International Studies in Educational Achievement)[1] in 1993 to be the most regularly used approach in elementary schools, mainly in the subject areas of mathematics and mother tongue; Europe appears to follow this trend. However, when we consider that this type of usage implies individual pupil access to a computer, it is evident that not many children have been able to benefit from CAI so far. Simple CAI packages usually consist of one or many sets of correction-incorporated worksheets, often providing recording facilities that enable the teacher to check on individual results. This in itself is a time-consuming task that adds to the work-load of the teacher, particularly when we consider that while one or two pupils are working on the computer, he or she is busy with the rest of the class. CAI is often used either for remedial work or for "brighter" pupils needing supplementary or "extension" exercises.

CAI+ software packages include options for recording the pupil's progress from one lesson to the next, as well as a range of levels for adaptation to pupils' needs. A test is often included to help the teacher place each pupil at the appropriate starting level, though sometimes this is done through input of reading or mathematical age. Computer Managed Instruction (CMI) programs offer all of the above capacities plus testing, analysis and diagnostic facilities and teaching modules. All programs in this category present the advantage of providing the learner with immediate feedback, though this can range from the simple "right" or "wrong" to a more complex diagnostic response in the more sophisticated CMI programs. A leading expert who runs the "La Villette - Cité des Enfants" in France had an amusing anecdote to tell in reference to feedback in what he calls "closed" learning environments characteristic (i.e. the exercises and answers are pre-set and leave no room for creativity) of most software in this category. He came across a group of children who seemed to be having far too much fun working with a sophisticated CAI program. After observing the

---

1. Pelgrum W.J., Plomp T., *The IEA Study of Computers in Education*, U.K., Pergamon Press, 1993, p. 122

highly computer-literate group for a few minutes he realised the object of their "learning activity" was to see who could produce the wrong answer that would take the computer the longest time to diagnose and give feedback! This appears to be a widespread practice. In *The Children's Machine: Rethinking School in the Age of the Computer*, Seymour Papert records a similar experience with American children.

"Clowns" - a CAI program for 4 - 8 year olds*

** *Clowns*, one of the programs included in the starting package distributed in the Comenius project in the Netherlands, is intended to complement existing materials used to train the functional development of infants. It consists of nine strands differing in content and purpose - these deal with perception of colour and shape, visual discrimination and analysis, visual synthesis, concept formation, oral usage and precision development of the motor system. Each of these strands comprise several levels of difficulty: cognitive levels range from 1-10, and motor levels 1-5. The only direct feedback is the clown which appears on the screen from time to time as a reward. *Clowns* offers supplementary practice "sheets" and recording facilities (the results of the work session and the pupil's cognitive and motor level are recorded but overwritten each time the child begins a new session), as well as a possibility for teachers to add their own exercises. It is up to the teacher to use the registered results to make his own analyses.

This program provides teachers with a creative tool to stimulate functional development and, because they are free to decide which strands and which level of the program are adapted to the needs of each pupil, to give the individualised "teaching" that is so important at this early stage, since children have often had very different learning experiences and are consequently at very different functional levels when they begin school. The self-instructive, self-corrective character of the program makes it particularly useful for work with special needs pupils.

To use *Clowns*, children must comprehend the basics of colour and shape, be able to perceive visually, concentrate on one task for a certain period of time and use a mouse, a rich learning task in itself since it implies a considerable degree of eye-hand co-ordination. Children work at the computer individually or in pairs, beginning their work session by introducing themselves to the program by means of a picture code. The program provides a colourful and creative environment for children to become acquainted with IT and leads them to discover, often for the first time, the relationship between their own actions and the screen's reaction. Young learners also gain experience in working independently and at their own pace.

---

* 4-8 year olds refers to mental, and not chronological, age
** A large part of the information included in the next few paragraphs was provided by PRINT, the national IT implementation team set up in the framework of the Comenius operation.

Use of this program requires considerable effort on the teacher's behalf. Not only must he or she have a reasonable operating knowledge of Windows, particularly if he wants to input additional exercises, he must also be familiar with the content of all strands and levels included in the program before introducing it in class. He must use his own tests to determine the cognitive and motor level of his pupils. Some form of pupil guidance is obviously necessary at the beginning, though this can be handled by volunteer assistants, usually parents. If the teacher wishes to record results in order to make his own analysis of pupil progress, he must do so immediately after each session as these will be overwritten in the next session. Moreover, as *Clowns* is used individually or in pairs, class organisation must be given special consideration.

A number of enterprising primary school teachers throughout Europe, intent on giving pre-readers and young children with difficulties in learning to read access to the colourful, stimulating learning environment that the computer can offer, have produced their own software based on a similar approach to *Clowns*. One teacher (at last a woman!) working in the south of France has produced a CD-ROM, "Les Imbattables" (the Unbeatables), comprising 100 games for 5-7 year-olds and including strands in basic mathematics, geometry and logic. An IT co-ordinator in Italy, Mr Casamenti - I have introduced him by name as you will encounter him several times throughout these pages -, makes his own reading readiness software especially adapted for children struggling to learn Italian. Through print-out facilities, these children can also handle the shapes and objects they see on the screen as a means of consolidating the learning process, or inversely as a means of preparing for their first computer sessions.

QUANTOFA - learning to calculate in columns

This software is another of Mr Casamenti's creations. In Italy, few special needs schools exist; children with learning difficulties and physical disabilities usually attend mainstream education establishments. The wide diversity of input and output devices that can be attached to a computer make this medium very attractive for teachers trying to provide equal learning opportunities for the whole class. This particular software can be used with a head-sensor or a lead foot.

Saint Giovanni school has, through the efforts of teachers, parents and the local municipality, been equipped with a computer laboratory containing five computers, a printer and an electronic communication link. Each class has access to the computer laboratory once a week. The class is split into two for this type of activity, the two groups taking turns to work at the machines for half-hour sessions. One of the advantages of this type of organisation is that pupils know that their time is limited; efforts are particularly intense during the half-hour on the computer, but concentration and motivation remain high in the off-time too, because children are busy consolidating work from the last session

On-site Observation
GRID N° 1

SCHOOL/CLASS:	S. Giovanni - Italy - grades 3, 4, 5
DATE:	04/05/1996
RELEVANCE OF IT:	Present calculating activity as a game, improve abilities & techniques in maths, particularly for children with learning difficulties
PROGRAM USED:	QUANTOFA, to teach math calculations in columns. Designed by a teacher in the school, produced by a parent programmer
COMPUTER DISTRIBUTION:	5 computers in lab, class (usually 20 - 25 pupils) is divided into 2 groups; pupils take turns to work in pairs for 1/2 hour sessions, one day per week
DEGREE OF INTERACTION ALLOWED BY SOFTWARE:	Chn work in pairs according to learning levels, there is a high degree of solidarity. They help each other to overcome difficulties
VARIETY OF ACTIVITIES TAKING PLACE SIMULTANEOUSLY:	Half the class works on computer with one teacher, the other half usually works on consolidation or creative activities with another teacher
TEACHER PURPOSE (3 CULTURES):	To develop computer-literacy as a means of problem-solving
GROUP WORK/TEAM SPIRIT:	Pair interaction is most satisfactory; chn are motivated, enthusiastic, happy
SENSE OF RESPONSIBILITY/ PERSONAL DISCIPLINE:	Particularly high during computer sessions, beneficial effects are also noted outside the computer lab. Operations & print out on computer take less time than they do with notebooks
DEGREE OF DECISION-MAKING/COMMITMENT/WILLINGNESS TO TAKE RISKS:	Self-confidence is developed, chn have a real desire to go ahead & finish what the computer asks of them
SENSE OF INITIATIVE/ CURIOSITY/CREATIVITY:	A noted improvement in autonomy in learning
DEGREE OF ATOMISATION/ SOCIALISATION:	Solidarity is high between partners
SENSE OF ACHIEVEMENT/ PRIDE IN WORK:	Self-esteem increases, particularly in pupils with learning difficulties
CORRESPONDENCE TO PURPOSE/LEVEL OF ACHIEVEMENT IN CULTURE:	The result of the activity corresponds to the objectives & expectations of teacher

The 3 cultures refer to: humanities; mathematics, science and technology; economic and social issues, as described in Cochinaux P., *Moving Towards Learning Society*, Louvain, CRE-ERT, 1995, p. 12.

Background Grid page 137.

and preparing for the next one - they don't want to lose a second of precious computer time because their work has been poorly organised.

The content of this software is presented in the form of games that lead even maths-allergic pupils to tackle their exercises enthusiastically. Children appear to work faster than when using the traditional pen and notepad; learning is apparently more vivid since children retain what they have learned, and refer to *QUANTOFA* when they are confronted with a related problem outside of the computer laboratory. Obviously task-specific software can only be used for a very limited period of time with the same class, however, this problem is overcome by the fact that, as Mr Casamenti is the IT co-ordinator for eight schools, the teaching programs of all of these are co-ordinated so that software can be passed around. This is just one of a dozen or so "home-grown" products being used by the eight schools.

A computer managed instruction program

The National Council of Educational Technology (NCET), a government-funded organisation responsible for introducing IT in England, has been attributed the mission of setting up and assessing pilot projects on specific types of IT utilisation in order to determine the most effective means of ameliorating the teaching/learning process. The NCET also produces its own software, teaching material, brochures and the teacher training courses (in conjunction with relevant training establishments) necessary to launch the implementation of IT on a national scale. It runs its own telematic server which provides a valuable source of information on projects underway and IT resources available, and regularly publishes catalogues to keep teachers and educational authorities up to date on available software. One Computer Managed Instruction project run by the NCET is described below.

The *Integrated Learning System*[2] (ILS) project began in answer to a newspaper advertisement from an American software publisher seeking European schools to test its comprehensive CMI program. The NCET examined the concept, decided that it could be suitable for use in UK schools, and has, since early 1994, set up a total of 16 pilot sites for children of ages 7 - 11 years. The system is based on a Freinet-type approach whereby children work for half an hour per day at their own rhythm and at their own level on the large store of correction-incorporated worksheets included in the software. Entry level is set by initial placement tests which demand of the class teacher both a precise knowledge of the capacities of each of his pupils, and of the contents of the system in the three subject areas concerned - mathematics, reading and language development skills. Once the appropriate starting level has been determined, the children then work their way upwards with little teacher intervention and

---

2. NCET, *Integrated Learning Systems - a report of the pilot evaluations of ILS in the UK*, Coventry, NCET, 1994.

On-site Observation
GRID N° 2

SCHOOL/CLASS:	Parkhill Primary School - UK - KS1+ KS2 (8 pupils)
DATE:	05/06/1995
RELEVANCE OF IT:	Use of ILS to develop skills of independent learning. Diagnostic facilities and worksheets enable tchr to integrate ILS work with class work
PROGRAM USED:	Integrated Learning System (CMI)
COMPUTER DISTRIBUTION:	4 computers are placed on a central raised "island" surrounded by 3 separate classrooms where teachers are working with rest of each class
DEGREE OF INTERACTION ALLOWED BY SOFTWARE:	Simple question/answer type drills (with sound) allowing little real interaction except for feedback. Children work at their own level & rhythm after initial placement tests
VARIETY OF ACTIVITIES TAKING PLACE SIMULTANEOUSLY:	Child works via computer through worksheets on mathematics, reading & language development skills
TEACHER PURPOSE (3 CULTURES):	To consolidate and continue learning process in core subjects - mathematics & humanities
GROUP WORK/TEAM SPIRIT:	non-applicable
SENSE OF RESPONSIBILITY/ PERSONAL DISCIPLINE:	All 8 students (six 7yr-olds + two 9yr-olds) showed a highly developed sense of responsibility & discipline in auto-management of their 1/2 hr daily time slot and of their progress
DEGREE OF DECISION-MAKING/COMMITMENT/WILLINGNESS TO TAKE RISKS:	The computer decides, not the child, but chn are highly committed and take risks as they know computer will correct them & explain why - only 1 child was taken off ILS for disruptive behaviour
SENSE OF INITIATIVE/ CURIOSITY/CREATIVITY:	Chn take initiative to go on with new work, creativity is evident in chn's approach to solve new problems in their own way.
DEGREE OF ATOMISATION/ SOCIALISATION:	Chn work individually but show great social maturity in discussions with tchrs & by assuming their own responsibilities. Subsequent classwork makes up for lack of socialisation
SENSE OF ACHIEVEMENT/ PRIDE IN WORK:	Very high, proud to have been chosen for this pilot project (pilot group was chosen at random); noticeable improvement in behaviour of under-achievers
CORRESPONDENCE TO PURPOSE/LEVEL OF ACHIEVEMENT IN CULTURE:	Except for problem of Americanisation in language tasks, material is highly appropriate to purpose

Background grid page 138.

immediate feedback during and after each session. The major advantage of this system is that children work autonomously and become responsible for their own learning and for the management of their own time; the seven-year olds taking part in the project (limited to 8 out of a class of 30 due to a lack of equipment, but also as a means of measuring learning gains achieved through use of ILS) showed a highly-developed sense of responsibility in the way they kept a watch on the time and quietly left their class without having to be reminded by the teacher when it was "their turn" on the roster.

One of the great advantages of *Integrated Learning Systems*, as indeed with most other programs included in this category, is that the machine frees the teacher of his role of "judge", leaving him more time to devote to pupils requiring individualised attention, as well as to other more challenging tasks. Because of this, but also because they are relieved of the stress of teacher waiting for their response, pupils tend to take greater risks in trying to find an answer, confident in the knowledge that the computer will correct them and explain where they went wrong. No matter how long pupils take in giving their answer, they will receive immediate (and confidential) feedback. Moreover, because their errors are immediately spotted, they do not continue reinforcing them.

The Integrated Learning System includes a facility which enables the class teacher to keep individual records of progress, hence making report marks more meaningful. It also opens up unprecedented testing, analysis and diagnostic possibilities. An incorporated relational data base enables the teacher to analyse past lesson content and plan future lessons that can be used to integrate "computer" work into "class" work. In the schools in which *Integrated Learning Systems* are being used, teachers report a drop in absenteeism, an improvement in behaviour and an increase in motivation, particularly in underachievers. However, they also made note that use of such a system requires an appreciable effort in terms of specific teacher training, ongoing dialogue with the publisher and teacher trainers, and support from staff (often in other schools) who have found themselves confronted with similar problems. Being an American system, lengthy explanations on currency and spelling must be incorporated into class work before the introduction of the program. These aspects still cause more than a little frustration for young learners already struggling to master the keyboard and acquaint themselves to learning in interaction with a strongly pronounced American accent blurting through adult-sized headphones. It goes without saying that teachers are eagerly awaiting the appearance of a British version.

Control technology

In the category "control technology", we include object-oriented programming (mainly LOGO or, in one primary school in France, Smalltalk), simulation and modelling. Few programs are available for primary levels in either of the latter two as the high cost of task-oriented software puts it out of reach of most schools, particularly if the cost of translation is to be taken into consideration. Control technology enables pupils to act directly upon an object or an environment: the most extensively used technologies of this type are LOGO, floor turtles and/or roamers, all mainly prescribed for the subject area of mathematics, though they produce considerable learning gains in other areas too. More versatile control technology construction kits from "Control LEGO" and "Fischer Technics" provide the means for pupils to "build" their own experiments; NCET has recently developed a "contact" software kit that has now been marketed by a private publisher for the same purpose. Construction kits are once again used mainly to develop concepts in the areas of mathematics or science, however, because of their importance in the development of the reasoning process, this type of program in the hands of competent teachers succeeds in breaking down the artificial boundaries that divide subject areas on the curriculum.

Control technology basically provides a problem-solving environment in which pupils can make things happen, learn about cause and effect and even design tasks. Through the use of object-oriented languages such as LOGO or Smalltalk, described in the section below, the pupil becomes involved in a miniature world which is made up of several objects functioning in relation with each other within a same system. In designing a task, the pupil is, in fact, creating and testing a formal description of a process that will naturally lead him to consider, on the one hand, the properties of the constituents and, on the other, the expression of interactions. In the process he will incorporate a whole range of procedures essential to adult life - basic skills such as comparison, opposition, classification, transformation, combination and formulation of possibilities, as well as basic problem-solving skills, i.e. setting about finding the required information, knowing how and where to find this information and deciding on the right method to use. Testing the result of a design entails yet other skills such as approximation and estimation[3]. Problem-solving not only aids in the development of the higher mental processes of conceptualisation, induction, deduction and inference, it also enables the learner to construct methods of analysing and dealing with complex systems, which he can use in other domains.

LOGO, a simple computer language designed to give children an initial experience in programming, was particularly popular with primary school

---

3. CERI, *Information Technologies and Basic Learning*, Paris, OECD, 1987, p. 249

teachers throughout the eighties, perhaps because computer technology at that time was out of reach of all but the most enthusiastic users, who firmly believed that programming was the first step to computer use. Besides, few other "open-ended" programs suitable for primary school use were available until the late eighties or early nineties, and even today applications in mathematics are for the most part limited to CAI-type software. In his book *The Children's Machine: Rethinking School in the Age of the Computer*, Seymour Papert gives us an amusing insight into the problems of the way in which mathematics are taught at school; his major criticism is concisely summed up with a quote he says to have taken from both Voltaire and Nobel Prize winner Herbert Simon: "The best is the enemy of the good' - that is to say, the problem with school learning is the very little room it leaves for vague truths". LOGO offers an alternative to the right/wrong/wrong/right rhapsody that we still subject our children to during math lessons, not without cause since if one teacher is to "teach" thirty children, he or she has little time to do more than to correct an answer.

But even a correct answer does not necessarily imply that the child has understood the process and will be able to reproduce it or transfer it to real-life situations. One of the underlying objectives in the introduction of modern mathematics was the idea that, by introducing children to the notion of sets in the primary school and by developing a greater understanding of numeracy and basic mathematical processes, they would be better able to transfer their skills and knowledge to solve new problems[4]. LOGO corresponds to this objective in that each learner develops his own way of thinking and his own methodology to achieve the task he has set himself, whether this be to program a turtle to turn in a square, to write a program to make the lights inside a LEGO-built house flick on and off[5], or to create a Mickey Mouse head with squares and circles as we will see in the section on Smalltalk. In object-oriented programming, if the learner is to succeed in his task, he must express his ideas clearly and precisely, otherwise the computer cannot carry out his instructions. And because the program blindly obeys instructions to the very letter, he will sharpen his ability to spot errors and become aware of replacement strategies. In the "doing" process the child will gradually come to understand and use general concepts such as procedures, variables, functions and recursion. LOGO also provides practice in the mastery of the heuristic methods mentioned earlier e.g. planning and breaking down problems[6].

Problem-solving environments such as those described above have always existed in the classes of enterprising teachers, the difference today is that IT programs provide a ready-made environment that multiply the capacity of the

---

4. CERI, *Information Technologies and Basic Learning*, Paris, OECD, 1987, p. 242
5. Papert S., *The Children's Machine: Rethinking School in the Age of the Computer*, New York, Harvester/Wheatsheaf, 1993, p. 172
6. Feurzeig W., Algebra Slaves and Agents in a LOGO-based Mathematics Curriculum, *Instructional Science*, 14, 1986, p. 229-254

On-site Observation
GRID N° 3

SCHOOL/CLASS:	Cantona Elementary School - Italy - grade 3
DATE:	23/05/1996
RELEVANCE OF IT:	Use of computer to experiment with programming activities as a means of encouraging the development of cognitive capacities
PROGRAM USED:	LOGOWRITER
COMPUTER DISTRIBUTION:	7 computers in lab., separated into "islands"
DEGREE OF INTERACTION ALLOWED BY SOFTWARE:	Chn can work together to practice activity-planning, organisation in logical and temporal sequences, problem-solving using a "Top Down" methodology - a problem-solving-type cognitive process
VARIETY OF ACTIVITIES TAKING PLACE SIMULTANEOUSLY:	Pupils all work on computers at same time, pre-designed worksheets are given for extra activities
TEACHER PURPOSE (3 CULTURES):	Consolidate & develop concepts in geometry, logic & linguistics; reflect on knowledge construction process by observing chn's problem-solving strategies
GROUP WORK/TEAM SPIRIT:	The work is based on collective activities, divided into work units allocated to each group. Chn work together exchanging knowledge & exploring in a real climate of collaboration
SENSE OF RESPONSIBILITY/ PERSONAL DISCIPLINE:	Chn are highly motivated to work autonomously & attentively, knowing that their unit is an important element of the overall class activity - the functional importance of their own efforts for the advancement of the group
DEGREE OF DECISION-MAKING/COMMITMENT/WILLINGNESS TO TAKE RISKS:	The work consists of a progressive construction in which chn continually make operational decisions. Computer gives feedback enabling them to see their mistakes & learn from them
SENSE OF INITIATIVE/ CURIOSITY/CREATIVITY:	Chn continually use initiative to make hypotheses on solution paths they must try to verify. Chn design their own small projects on what other pupils have done
DEGREE OF ATOMISATION/ SOCIALISATION:	Chn work in small groups, presenting & discussing input with others and commenting on projects from other classes, strategies implemented and the results achieved
SENSE OF ACHIEVEMENT/ PRIDE IN WORK:	The result of the exercise can be communicated to and used by others (e.g. tales in Storygames). By being able to criticise the work of others, chn develop their own self-confidence
CORRESPONDENCE TO PURPOSE/LEVEL OF ACHIEVEMENT IN CULTURE:	The software meets teacher objective & provides a learning environment rich in potential

Background grid page 139.

teacher to provide rich learning experiences for all. Because IT cuts down on the time needed to build a model or simulate an experiment, children can start their task several times if they are unhappy with their results. Response time is also much shorter - feedback is now almost immediate. But, due to the shortened response time, will volatility of response become an element to be taken into consideration? What will be the residual benefit then? Will frequent utilisation be necessary if the child is not to forget? This brings us back to the question: "Is there a minimum IT access threshold below which children will not make sustainable learning gains?"

Object-oriented programming

Several projects were encountered in object-oriented programming, perhaps the most imaginative is one conducted by Mr Casamenti, our IT co-ordinator in Italy. He encourages teachers in his eight schools to introduce LOGO to their pupils through "body-LOGO" and by the use of statuettes. Children work in pairs or small groups, one or several of them taking on the role of "programmer" whilst another takes the role of the object being oriented. The programmer calls his instructions to the "object" who must blindly obey - FORWARD 1, TURN LEFT 90... The results are hilarious and the learning process so vivid that young learners are not ready to forget their first experience of LOGO, or the geometric concepts they discover.

LOGO Writer is another, more sophisticated version of object-oriented programming used in Italy, particularly popular because it is one of the very few educational programs for small children translated into Italian. Children select an object and their learning task opens with a written text that places the learner in the LOGO environment. Activities are numerous - children can find themselves in a field where their turtle must pick lettuce, in a maze in search of a way out, or architects of a castle. Programming takes place through the use of letters and numbers to convey instructions: A 2 (avanti 2 = forward 2), S 90 (turn left 90)...

However, in most countries it seems that LOGO has lost the aura of importance it was given in the eighties. Nowadays when you ask to see LOGO in action, teachers hasten to speak of telematic links or CD-ROM. Furthermore, few teachers dare to tackle even the simplest form of programming, as few feel they have had the necessary training. It should be pointed out that most teachers now using IT in class have developed their interest in new technology through personal use, which would almost definitely not include LOGO or programming of any type.

In a classroom in France, we were able to observe another form of object-oriented programming in action. *Smalltalk, un jeu d'enfant* (originally based on studies carried out in the late seventies at the Xerox Palo Alto Research Center

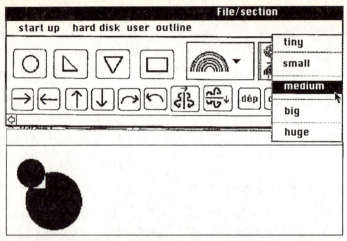

Making an ear : medium, round, black.

The object is copied, moved, coloured.

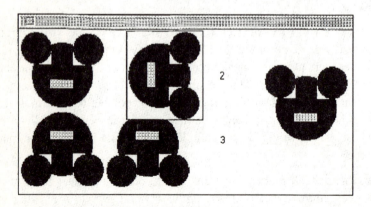

SCREENS FROM *SMALLTALK, UN JEU D'ENFANT*

in California) provides an attractive, colourful environment for young children to discover geometric concepts and work with objects that are motivating and familiar to them (train, dove, Mickey Mouse...). At one time, Smalltalk was seen as a possible successor to LOGO, though few concrete applications were ever developed. This French version of Smalltalk, developed by I. Borne and C. Girardot, enables children to design their own "wall paper" with an object of their choice using a roll-down menu of geometric actions: "move to the top/bottom/left/right", "turn 90", "vertical/horizontal symmetry". *Smalltalk, un jeu d'enfant* also provides a module for children to invent their own verb conjugation classifications. We have not gone into a description of the verb module here as it applies specifically to the French language.

An extension of the wallpaper module allows children to create their own object with circles, triangles and rectangles, choose a colour or simply design by outline. One inventive group chose to use this module to make their wallpaper with the head of Mickey Mouse - a combination of one large circle for the head, two small circles for the ears (they discovered that, as each design is on a square tile, by placing the ear-circle tiles in a certain spot they could leave blank triangles for the eyes) and a pink rectangle for the mouth. But when they began turning Mickey around to make the overall wallpaper design, they suddenly came upon an unpleasant surprise. Their object was wider horizontally than vertically. An animated discussion took place to discover why. Through the use of Smalltalk these young learners are actively involved in the process of discovering geometry, formalising the underlying concepts of mathematics in an amusing way that would not have been possible without IT. Moreover, the highly creative, aesthetic environment breaks down technical barriers that often frighten the more artistic pupils, allowing them to combine art and technology, to bridge the gap between the two cultures[7]. It seems particularly important to underline this fact; programs of this type provide unique aesthetic and creative opportunities in a curriculum and a world that is leaving progressively less room for all that is not purely "rational".

In the second part of the exercise, children are to use the object they have chosen or created in repeated geometrical translations to make a wallpaper design consisting of a minimum of four positions. Once they have mastered the technique and understood all the options available on roll-down menus, they are asked to write their own step-by-step program on paper (due to the lack of computers, only two of the seven groups can work on the computer at once). Pupils are led to hypothesise about the next step that will continue the pattern they have chosen. Through the formulation of hypotheses and experimentation, they are developing problem-solving strategies that can be transferred to other situations. Not only are they actively discovering geometry in their artistic

7. Papert S., *The Children's Machine: Rethinking School in the Age of the Computer*, New York, Harvester/Wheatsheaf, 1993, p. 124.

On-site Observation
GRID N° 4

SCHOOL/CLASS:	School annexe to IUFM - France - Tchr: G. Bonnerat
DATE:	30/05/1995
RELEVANCE OF IT:	Design of wallpaper squares to discover geometrical concepts & later to write own programs
PROGRAM USED:	Smalltalk - un jeu d'enfant; module used - "Design by sections"
COMPUTER DISTRIBUTION:	One computer & colour printer for a class of 27, each group of 3 takes turns to use computer for a total of 4 x 1/2 or 3/4 hour sessions
INTERACTION ALLOWED BY SOFTWARE:	Open choice of "object" leads to lively discussion from outset. Children are left to discover menu & possibilities available. Interaction taking place: pupil/pupil, pupil/computer &, after print-out, group/rest of class.
VARIETY OF ACTIVITIES TAKING PLACE SIMULTANEOUSLY:	Children are working on 2 of the 3 available modules of software: making wallpaper design through combination of geometrical shapes or with motifs provided (clown, dove, train...)
TEACHER PURPOSE (3 CULTURES):	Mathematics - create an attractive repetitive design through discovery of geometrical concepts (symmetry, rotation, translation to another position)
GROUP WORK/TEAM SPIRIT:	Motivation & team spirit aided by need for artistic & mathematical input, leads to interesting observation that artistic expression can overcome aversion to mathematics & technology (cf Papert).
SENSE OF RESPONSIBILITY/ PERSONAL DISCIPLINE:	With just 3 chn per group, each is important in group output. Chn totally absorbed by task in hand & anxious to make most of short time allocation on computer
DEGREE OF DECISION-MAKING/COMMITMENT/WILL INGNESS TO TAKE RISKS:	Task is totally directed by children, who realise importance of choice of design that they are to "manipulate". An initial lesson on general features of computer & disks shows they have leeway to take risks
SENSE OF INITIATIVE/ CURIOSITY/CREATIVITY:	Options on menu bar offer wide possibilities to awaken curiosity; a manipulation often gives totally unexpected results (rotation 90° lays clown on his nose)
DEGREE OF ATOMISATION/ SOCIALISATION:	Many opportunities through group work & class presentations. Children learn to criticise constructively & to clearly explain a procedure step-by-step
SENSE OF ACHIEVEMENT/ PRIDE IN WORK:	Use of colour printer (displayed on overhead projector) provides for production of aesthetic wallpapers that are even more attractive than on-screen
CORRESPONDENCE TO PURPOSE/LEVEL OF ACHIEVEMENT IN CULTURE:	Chn are actively & interactively exploring geometry & programming

Background grid page 140.

creation, they are also thinking about the syntax of their programming language and being introduced to concepts specific to the language of objects.

From these observations, we can draw the conclusion that IT object-oriented programs have definitely enhanced the teaching of basic geometrical concepts. And, as Plato said, "A basic education in geometry enables a child to situate himself in relation to the world and to space". Without a basic knowledge of geometry, could we recognise symbols or read a road map? It is a pity to note that, to date, *Smalltalk* is still only being used on an experimental basis in one pilot school in France, largely due to lack of funds. The two computers used during this project were on loan from Apple Computers. The class observed is in a school attached to the local teacher training college.

Modelling and simulation

Whereas modelling is an expressive action to create parameters in a partly bounded domain in order to make a virtual world that is a replica (though perhaps reduced or enlarged in size) of the real one, simulation is limited to an exploratory action - the model is fixed but the user can, by modifying one or more factors, modify the world that is represented. Both are problem-solving environments used mainly in the field of science, mathematics and geography, to a greater extent in secondary than primary education because of the cost of software and the fact that use is restricted to highly specific topics within a subject area, e.g. mechanics, electricity and magnetism, ecology, road traffic[8]. Although during this study we were able to observe no more than one or two rather limited examples of this type of software, it seems important to make mention of simulation and modelling in this report since both provide a unique environment in which learners are forced to express explicit internalised models that cannot be currently accessed in other kinds of teaching. Human interaction is so ambiguous that there is little opportunity, particularly at school where the class teacher usually has the responsibility of up to 30 pupils, for the learner and the teacher to clearly discern the form of an individual's cognitive models[9]. Perhaps more attention should be focused on this area during primary education, at a time when pupils are modifying, reorganising and adding to the cognitive models that will serve them in all future learning. IT provides a major advantage in this area since the computer-child interaction can, to a certain extent, replace the teacher-pupil interaction, thereby multiplying the teacher's capacity to cater to class needs.

Because of the complexity of the numerous relations involved and the often unforseeable character of their effects in the real situations represented in simulation and modelling, the learner is confronted with a problem-solving

8. Ogborn J., The Role of Modelling in Science Education, in the Final Report of the 45th European Teachers' Seminar, *Information Technology in Science Education*, Council of Europe, 1989, p. 13 - 23,
9. Lewis R., The Contribution of Information Technologies to Learning, in the Final Report of the 45th European Teachers' Seminar, *Information Technology in Science Education*, Council of Europe, 1989, p. 5-11

situation in which he is forced to express his beliefs through action. The computer serves as a mirror in "acting out" the consequences of these beliefs. In this way the learner assumes the consequences of his decisions and is led to discover the underlying rules in a scientific-type process, hence acquiring an intuitive idea of the way underlying principles determine various situations[10]. Through programs of this type, IT is preparing the ground for the development of a "research" reasoning mode, a reasoning mode formerly attained only by an intellectual elite who reached the upper level of university studies where "learning by research" becomes a prerequisite (e.g. for PhD students).

The ImpacT Report[11] relates an interesting account of the use of simulation software in a geography class in the context of Third-world studies with thirty-one 12-14 year-old pupils in a secondary school in the UK. The software, INDIAN FARMER represents the life of a farming family in India. On-screen the pupils encounter and actually become the members of an Indian farming family, having to make momentous decisions such as whether to sell a cow, get married, or leave the farm to move to the city. From the comments recorded - "Oh God, not another baby"; "We've got ourselves out of debt!" - we can see that the pupils were experiencing "first-hand" the life of an Indian farmer with a vividness that could not be achieved by even the best of teachers. Moreover, by living out the consequences of their decisions in an environment in which geography, nature, science, mathematics and humanities are creatively but realistically linked, they begin to become aware of the interconnections that exist in their own life between areas seemingly far-removed. Researchers on the project reported that, as a direct result of the simulation experience, pupils developed a greater awareness of demographic problems, the significance of the healthiness of their diet and the difficulty of moving out of the poverty/debt cycle. By developing awareness of the interconnections existing between all aspects of life and by leading the learner to discover that even the most minor decision can have major effects in seemingly unrelated areas, perhaps IT is giving rise to new reflexes that will gradually become incorporated in the decision-making process. If this is the case, IT is serving as a decision-making aid that will enable future citizens to make better decisions (optimal in statistical terms) when confronted with situations that call for increasingly rapid responses in a world that is ever more complex.

The object of this and four similar "Third-world" simulation projects carried out by the King's College for the ImpacT Report was to assess pupil-attitude and learning gains. All pupils concerned showed a marked increase in motivation, interest, concentration and involvement, which pupils themselves contributed to the fact that the simulations challenged their knowledge base by placing them in a context in which the detail was greater and more complex than

10. CERI, *Information Technologies and Basic Learning*, Paris, OECD, 1987, p. 260
11. This section is almost entirely based on Cox M., Johnson D.C., *The ImpacT Report*, London, King's College, 1993, p. 61-76

hitherto experienced. Learners reported that they had found the work inherently challenging because it involved real choice. Teachers noted a vast improvement in collaborative and communicative skills, the project providing a focused and structured vehicle for group work in which even "non-high-fliers" could offer a hypothesis that the group would consider. Once again, it was noted that this type of program, and the use of IT in general, provided a new route for learning by encouraging interaction between pupils, initiating them in the art of consultation, co-operation and complementarity. Each one was naturally allocated a role corresponding to his particular capacities, hence enabling each member to make a worthy contribution to the efforts of the team in making decisions.

The only software[12] of this type that I discovered during the present study was a simulation software program called *At Home in the Environment*, included in the Comenius (see chapter on Implementation) starter package made available to all schools participating in the Netherlands. This program basically concerns geography, nature studies and world studies, and is intended to assist pupils (11-12 year-olds) in acquiring knowledge of environmental concepts and in gaining awareness of these in the immediate surroundings (e.g. waste and energy consumption in home and school). The computer program is part of a kit that includes content for instruction and discussion as well as suggestions for activities that will help pupils internalise concepts being learnt - "learning by doing". The software contains a question section (which can be turned off if the teacher wishes) and a simulation program that takes at least half an hour (facilities are available for setting a time-limit). It is intended for individual or pair work.

In this package, pupils must decide how to dispose of garbage in the home or the school. They must incorporate data acquired through teacher instruction, from maps and from symbols they have been given denoting different types of waste, and from the national environmental bill. If garbage is dumped in the wrong way, the game is over on that day at midnight and the household starts from scratch again. Besides all the previously mentioned advantages in terms of learning gains that simulation software can bring, this particular problem-solving environment promotes awareness of environmental issues and underlines the importance of individual decisions on the general well-being of the community.

We shall now take a look at the "Thinking gains" in terms of valued kinds of thinking (I find the term "reasoning" more appropriate in this context) that participants at the 45th Council of Europe Teachers' Seminar ("The impact of the new technologies in the teaching of science") defined as arising from the use of simulation and modelling at all education levels:

---

12. Thanks are extended to the staff of Print for the information included on At home in the environment.

- *Active* thinking directed to a goal, asking "why"; guessing, predicting
- *Critical* thinking about the limits of models and consequences
- *Abstracting* from the concrete, simplifying, idealising, recognising funda-
mentals, relating to real-life experiences
- *Selecting*, organising, interpreting information
- *Imagining* possible worlds; changing their rules
- *Perceiving* forms of behaviour, (similarities, analogues)[13]

These "Thinking gains" correspond closely to the basic objectives of primary education discussed in Chapter 1. What IT has brought to the process is that it has rendered more accessible a scientific reasoning mode which, until now, was out of the reach of most learners. Teachers have always used scale models to explain how things work, enabling children to touch, explore and learn by action. When they have the time or the material possibilities, most teachers attempt to take their classes out into the world to see the real thing. With IT, the real world can more easily be brought into the classroom; one scale model is replaced by as many models as there are computers in the room, providing access to all students simultaneously. Yet although the above-mentioned report was published in 1989, few simulation or modelling programs have been developed for use in primary education, largely due to cost. Should the cost of such programs be allowed to erect an eternal barrier between young learners and the new learning experiences we can provide?

Extending horizons for the physically handicapped

In the previous sections, we have closely examined the manner in which IT may provide a powerful means of overcoming certain reasoning "handicaps" that could prevent our citizens from developing full autonomy in practising their decision-making rights in the democracy of our nations. Approximately 2% of Western populations suffer from severe learning or physical handicaps which prevent them from attending mainstream schools. Now we shall consider the ways in which IT can be used to enable such children to develop a certain degree of autonomy by gaining greater control over their environment[14].

Control technology is, as we mentioned earlier, about making things happen; severely disabled people often have great difficulty in exercising any appreciable degree of control over their environment. IT offers a major advantage for such learners because of the wide range of input devices that can be used to enter data and hence to trigger a process. With IT children can work together, the capacities of one pupil compensating for the disabilities of another. Input devices can be adapted to suit the learner - symbol-to-word software for

---

13. Group Report, The Role of Computers for Modelling in Science Education, in the Final Report of the 45th European Teachers' Seminar, *Information Technology in Science Education*, Council of Europe, 1989, p. 41-45.
14. Hart B., Holt G., Fletcher C., Tyldesley A., *Extending Horizons*, U.K., NCET, 1994, Being in control

those unable to communicate in text, a foot pedal to replace the mouse for those who cannot use their arms, or a mouth piece for the severely maimed or limbless. The learner has the satisfaction of seeing (or hearing) the movement that he has triggered, thereby enabling him to link cause and effect. He can experience the satisfaction of having physical access to controlling activities. Moreover, as a non-judgmental medium, IT gives even the most timid learner the right to learn by trial and error, to experience success and failure and to develop his full learning potential. A report on the Extending Horizons project developed in the UK to cater to the difficulties of special needs pupils shows that control technology has opened new pathways to:

- more complete spatial awareness
- understanding of language structures
- simple problem-solving (including group problem-solving)
- improved social interaction

Results from a number of experiments carried out and still underway in the UK show that the use of control technology for children with severe learning difficulties can enhance the following basic and higher level skills[15]:

- neuro-motor control
- kinaesthetic awareness
- sequencing and logic
- language skills
- listening and recall
- decision-making
- collaborative group work
- roles and responsibilities
- enjoyment
- levels of concentration and social skills.

IT, particularly in control technology, is enabling a great many special needs children to be integrated into the mainstream educational system at last.

---

15. Hart B., Holt G., Fletcher C., Tyldesley A., Being in Control in *Extending Horizons*, U.K., NCET, 1994

Chapter 4

The wide applications
of general-purpose software

Expression and communication

Educational theorists, Piaget, Vygotsky, Bruner and Donaldson included, have long stressed the importance of developing in our pupils a fluent, articulate command of language if we are to foster the transition from concrete to formal operational reasoning[16]. Although nowadays it is generally accepted that logic arises from action, not language, verbal reasoning is a major vehicle or medium on which logical operations operate. Language provides the most important means by which a child can communicate his mental representations of scenarios and events, and have them received and examined, accepted or rejected, by others. Through a process of self-regulation, he will then gradually modify and build on his concepts and knowledge, and continue on his path of learning. Both written and oral expression therefore serve an important function, not only in the mastery of knowledge, but also in the development of reasoning and in communication in a social context.

D. Woods, an author recommended to most trainee teachers in English-speaking countries, points out that there are definite relations between literacy and the ability to reason in hypothetical, logical terms. He quotes studies showing that people from non-literate cultures have to date failed to give evidence of formal reasoning. He uses as a second example to consolidate this point of view the fact that although most very deaf children, those who are born deaf or become deaf before learning to talk, eventually learn to solve concrete operational problems, they never manage to solve formal operational ones, i.e. problems which involve abstract or hypothetical ideas. It is interesting to note that in Portugal a telematics project is underway in a school for the deaf to see if IT can serve to ameliorate communication skills. The results of this project are not yet available.

Socialisation, mentioned earlier as being one of the major roles of the school, also takes place through language; language is the vehicle by which we transmit the roots of our cultural heritage and communicate the norms and values of our society. In a society such as ours steeped in written tradition, reading and

---

16. Wood D., *How Children Learn and Think*, Oxford, UK, Blackwell, 1988, p. 148-149

writing are not only social acts, they also provide the key to all future learning. The school therefore has a major role to play in developing a high degree of literacy in each and every citizen if we are to provide equal opportunities for all.

Written expression, an essential element in literacy, has long fired debates in cultural, political and educational circles as to the way it should be taught in schools. For a long time, traditional methods placed the accent on correcting and commenting pupils' work, often discouraging creativity in the process. We then went through a period of avoiding too many corrections on one page; the result was that teachers were faced with a difficult choice of which errors to correct and which ones to leave uncorrected. Conscientious teachers were confronted with the task of keeping meticulous records of pupils' errors if they were to effectively follow progress and reach the desired goal; pupils went on reinforcing errors or, in the best of cases, tried to understand why an error one week, or on one pupil's work, went by uncorrected the next time. Oral expression, on the other hand, has earned little attention and is only too often "forgotten" due to the demands of a busy teaching schedule and the difficulties of measuring progress when it comes to assessment. Yet speech and listening skills are inherent to the process of written expression. The average worker spends 8.4% of his or her communication time at work writing, 13.3% reading, 23% speaking and 55% listening[17].

With the widespread availability of word-processing programs and, perhaps more importantly, the cost effectiveness of a software program that will serve for pupils of all ages in all subjects compared to task-oriented programs limited to a specific age range and a specific subject, word processing is being used in a great number of schools throughout Europe to develop and encourage written expression, particularly in group project work. This also corresponds to a recent trend in education which places a new emphasis on the mastery of the native language in the primary school, in an attempt to overcome the shortcomings that the educational system has been accused of in the past[18].

Word processing

In written expression, ideally the writer should generate, gather and organise his ideas, then refine and revise them until the desired result is obtained. The use of a computer in written expression enhances the learning process in that it does away with the physical discomfort of multiple rewriting and correction, thereby encouraging children to persevere until they are happy with their final result. It also facilitates self-correction, far more gratifying and efficient than teacher correction, by giving immediate feedback on spelling, vocabulary, structure, punctuation, grammar and style, and help on setting out documents by providing

17. Carnevale A.P., Skill and the New Economy, in *Gestion 2000*, 1992, N°4, p.155
18. Cochinaux, P., de Woot, P., *Moving Towards a Learning Society*, Geneva-Brussels, CRE-ERT, 1995, p.76-78.

models on which pupils can base their own work. The simplest of word processing programs usually contain a multitude of options that will encourage exploration in linguistic expression. No matter what difficulties children may have had in producing their composition, the final print-out will look almost professional - they are thus encouraged to take greater pride in their work. Teachers regularly using word-processing in class have noted that children write much longer compositions, and that motivation has greatly increased.

The blank screen of a computer provides an enhanced learning environment, even for children who are reticent to express themselves. Gerard Gretsch of the SCRIPT organisation (Co-ordination and Research Service for Pedagogical and Technical Innovation) in Luxembourg highlights two of the advantages of the use of the computer in written and oral expression in one of his recent publications: "Children see before them a screen and a keyboard (or icons) which offer a silent invitation to explore the universe of the written or recorded word[19]." And, on the subject of the delete key : "it avoids fear of error; it avoids frustration; it encourages the most timid to start typing; it encourages aesthetic research: ' I delete because it doesn't look good'; it allows an attitude of research: 'I try, assess, and delete if I'm not happy'; it incites pupils to seek perfection in page layout"[20].

Word processing provides a number of advantages for the teacher, too. It frees him to a large extent from the onerous task of correcting since his pupils have in their hands an efficient auto-correction tool; it overcomes the problem of illegible handwriting; work can be stored all year long and easily accessed on floppy disks to make the assessment of progress easier, more rapid and more effective.

This and other types of general-purpose software such as data-bases, spreadsheets and desktop publishers are proving particularly popular in countries such as Luxembourg where few tutoring-type software products are translated into the native language because of high translation costs and the limited size of the national market.

Communication through Wide Area Network links

Wide Area Network links are being used in some countries to take the communication process one step further, though not many schools are fortunate enough to have ready access to a telephone line or sufficient budget to cover the high cost of communications. In a Luxembourg project, primary school pupils have produced a newsletter in conjunction with schools in France and Canada; in the Bologna area in Italy thirty schools communicate regularly by e-mail and have attempted to set up connections with schools in other countries, though the

---

19. Gretsch G., TEO - *Développement et evaluation d'un traitement de texte orale*, Luxembourg, Ministère de l'Education Nationale, 1994,
20. Cohen R., *Quand l'Ordinateur Parle*, Paris, PUF, 1992, p.95,

language barrier often raises insurmountable problems for young children unless a few translators are on hand during e-mail sessions. Nevertheless, plans are still underway to set up a joint project with Genoa and Manchester for the exchange of information on environmental aspects in each of the areas (e.g. rivers, towns, smog, etc.).

Network links create a new language learning environment by bringing together a multi-national community of learners and providing for new social exchanges. Written expression takes on a new dimension when eager authors are sure that, at the end of the telephone line, they have an enthusiastic audience waiting to receive their "publications". Suddenly, because the content of written expression exercises takes on a new importance, pupils become aware of the fact that they must express themselves clearly if their ideas are not to be misunderstood by readers with whom they will never have the opportunity to dialogue. Through the necessary co-ordination of a multitude of cognitive skills, strategies and knowledge that are involved in the process of formal representation, pupils gradually begin to develop meta-cognitive knowledge i.e. the capacity to reflect upon their own knowledge[21].

TEO - an oral text processing software

Luxembourg has developed a most interesting piece of software called TEO (Traitement de l'expression orale) to process oral text in both native and foreign languages. This is the result of a Research and Development project realised jointly by SCRIPT and the national teacher training college ISERP. The software was produced by the Henri Tudor Centre for Public Research, with the assistance of the national Centre for Technology in Education.

TEO is presented in the form of a blank page similar to that used in word processing programs, with a traditional but simplified menu bar at the top of the screen and, at the bottom of the screen, a series of icons which, when activated, record a spoken sentence. Children work in groups of three or four at the machine, taking turns to choose an icon and record their sentence to build a story. When all of the sentences have been recorded, the pupils can rearrange or delete the icons as they wish until they have obtained a final product that is to their satisfaction. A number of stories have been regrouped on a CD-ROM which gives a remarkable insight into the desires, fears and taboos that children will express when working out of the reach of a teacher, even though they are fully aware that they will be required to present their story in class once it is finished.

The TEO software is a unique oral-expression progress tool in that it "captures" the speech of a child, enabling the teacher to keep a record of the

---

21. CERI, *Information Technologies and Basic Learning: Reading, Writing, Science and Mathematics*, Paris, OECD, 1987, p. 133

On-site Observation
GRID N° 5

SCHOOL/CLASS:	Altwies Primary - Luxembourg - 8-9 yr olds
DATE:	02/06/1995
RELEVANCE OF IT:	Use of oral text processing to build a story
PROGRAM USED:	TEO developed by Henri Tudor centre & SCRIPT
COMPUTER DISTRIBUTION:	One portable computer used in room adjoining classroom, 3 chn work at computer while class continues oral French lesson
INTERACTION ALLOWED BY SOFTWARE:	High degree of interaction, chn help each other, "talk" to computer, then use it as tool to rearrange language input into a story to be enjoyed by class
VARIETY OF ACTIVITIES TAKING PLACE SIMULTANEOUSLY:	Story-building, oral expression, dictionary skills for new words, negotiating for next sentence, mutual help and corrections are given
TEACHER PURPOSE (3 CULTURES):	Humanities - develop foreign language skills & confidence in oral work through group interaction
GROUP WORK/TEAM SPIRIT:	Chn choose group partners, work together enthusiastically because they share a common self-chosen story they wish to impart to the rest of class (and that may eventually be recorded on CD-ROM)
SENSE OF RESPONSIBILITY/ PERSONAL DISCIPLINE:	Given limited time-slot, chn discipline each other to present best ideas & structures possible - the class will later constructively criticise their work
DEGREE OF DECISION-MAKING/COMMITMENT/WILL INGNESS TO TAKE RISKS:	All decisions are up to chn - they have a blank screen & a selection of icons with which to work. They take risks by incorporating expressions & language they have heard or find in dictionary; they are totally committed to task in hand
SENSE OF INITIATIVE/ CURIOSITY/CREATIVITY:	High degree of all 3. Story can take any turn they wish (sometimes rather "osé"). Creative manipulation of icons (oral utterances) when input is complete to modify or improve story
DEGREE OF ATOMISATION/ SOCIALISATION:	High degree of collaboration between groups, social interaction during class presentations when they must handle class criticism
SENSE OF ACHIEVEMENT/ PRIDE IN WORK:	Chn are proud of their stories, but also of icon display they have chosen to represent it
CORRESPONDENCE TO PURPOSE/LEVEL OF ACHIEVEMENT IN CULTURE:	Even most timid are encouraged to express themselves orally. Peer-learning is high as certain chn are more familiar with foreign language than others

Background grid page 141.

child's progress by enabling him to compare new examples with earlier work. The children themselves become more aware of their own production and begin to permanently assess it; through auto-evaluation they become actively involved in the learning process, at the same time developing listening skills.

Like word processing, oral text processing plays an important role in the psychological development process as it allows the child to dissect his own utterance, rearranging, deleting and adding as he wishes. In this way it enables him to develop another, more abstract, form of thinking, disconnected from the concrete and direct experience[22] - access to and development of this mode of "decentred" or "disembedded thinking" is indispensable both in aiding a child to express himself coherently in public, and in developing the higher cognitive skills needed if he is to succeed in his school cursus.

One inherent advantage in the use of computer in oral/written expression is that, because of the limited number of computers, children necessarily work in groups, each using and integrating his own competencies which are necessarily different to that of other pupils. Children with greater capacities help their peers to reach a higher level by enabling them to bridge the "gap" between what they are capable of doing alone and what they can achieve with the assistance of others more knowledgeable or skilled than themselves[23]. This constitutes what Vygotsky defined as the Proximal Zone of Development, whereby a child's potential for learning is revealed and indeed is often realised in interactions with more knowledgeable others. Obviously, this factor comes into play in all group interactions, the computer is no more than a medium that facilitates exchanges and provides more numerous occasions for children to share a creative experience.

In the lesson observed on the use of TEO at the Attwies primary school in Luxembourg, the 8-9 year-old children were working in a foreign language - French. The program could, however, be used in any language and appears to open up new horizons as a model for use in the native language.

IT in a global, "open-ended" learning approach

The initial objective of this study was to examine how IT could be incorporated into a global teaching approach to develop the strategies of "learning to learn" that will enable our children to become independent life-long learners. This, of course, implied that pupils have regular access to IT equipment on a daily basis, and the time to discover and learn at their own pace. However, as the months wore on and we continued on our path through classrooms in Europe, it gradually became evident that few classes possessed the necessary means to offer pupils more than spasmodic access to IT, and that

22. Donaldson M., *Children's Minds*, Glasgow, Fontana Press, 1978, p.76
23. Wood D., *How Children Learn and Think*, Oxford, UK, Blackwell, 1988, p. 24-25

On-site Observation
GRID N° 6

SCHOOL/CLASS:	Crauthem Primary School - Luxembourg - Grade 6
DATE:	11/12/1995
RELEVANCE OF IT:	Encourage expression in individual self-chosen projects, screen provides "public" display for group interaction
PROGRAM USED:	Word processing - a simplified program of German origin
COMPUTER DISTRIBUTION:	4 computers in a semi-closed section of classroom, one computer near wall in open classroom, 17 children in class move over to computer when they wish & when computer is free
INTERACTION ALLOWED BY SOFTWARE:	Screen publicly displays work, chn are encouraged to move around to see what others are doing, conversing freely on each other's project
VARIETY OF ACTIVITIES TAKING PLACE SIMULTANEOUSLY:	Most chn are working on their own project: writing, searching for relevant material, typing, checking; 2 are discussing a newspaper article on French politics; 4 chn are preparing a presentation on generators; 4 chn are developing their own versions of a poem one of them has written
TEACHER PURPOSE (3 CULTURES):	Humanities/science: projects range from music, railways, cats, space shuttle
GROUP WORK/TEAM SPIRIT:	Originally considered a "difficult" class, after 1 1/2 years in an "open" classroom chn now collaborate in a mature manner giving help when asked, but showing a large degree of autonomy in their learning tasks
SENSE OF RESPONSIBILITY/ PERSONAL DISCIPLINE:	Very little teacher intervention, except when advice is asked for. Chn can freely use telephone in class if they need information from outside sources
DEGREE OF DECISION-MAKING/COMMITMENT/WILL INGNESS TO TAKE RISKS:	Highly committed to their projects which will last 2 or 3 months. Completely autonomous to make decisions, choose their own strategies
SENSE OF INITIATIVE/ CURIOSITY/CREATIVITY:	Well-developed sense of initiative as chn direct their own activities for most of the day. Creative approaches to task, one child contacted an editor to find out about author of a book he was working on
DEGREE OF ATOMISATION/ SOCIALISATION:	Although working on individual projects, an overall "happy-busy" environment is evident. No children are "left out"
SENSE OF ACHIEVEMENT/ PRIDE IN WORK:	Professional-standard productions, collected by teachers into brochures illustrated with Mac Quick Time digital photos & scanned images. Class collaborates regularly with other schools to produce newsletters
CORRESPONDENCE TO PURPOSE/LEVEL OF ACHIEVEMENT IN CULTURE:	Computer/modem/telephone are used to make learning a meaningful experience placed in a real-life context. Chn are competent and business-like

Background grid page 142.

few teachers had broken away from a traditional daily routine, broken up into formal lessons slots to cover all the core subjects imposed by the curriculum. Then I stumbled upon the Crauthem primary school at Roeser, in Luxembourg.

The class observed is fortunate enough to possess four computers (installed with a user-friendly German word processing program since most children understand German and few programs are translated into the native language of a country counting no more than 350,000 inhabitants), one printer, a Mac "Quick Time" camera for digital photos & scanned images, a modem and a telephone line - all this thanks to the tireless efforts of the class teacher, Mr Fiermonte, the enthusiastic support and fund-raising activities of parents in the community and the supportive attitude of the head teacher. At Crauthem, IT has been incorporated into daily classroom routine in what can be considered as a truly global, open-ended approach to learning.

Disenchanted with traditional methods of teaching which he never really believed in the first place, Mr Fiermonte describes his role in the classroom as leader, counsellor and mentor, responsible for providing a rich environment in which pupils will become aware of their own centres of interest, learning objectives and the most appropriate means of achieving these. His top priority is to provide individualised attention for each pupil, adopting a differentiated approach that will cater to the needs of each and every one. He sees himself as no expert in computing, but can count on certain pupils to come up with solutions to technical problems - "We learn together". Above all, he considers it his role to "keep his finger on the pulse" of each child by making regular assessment of individual progress and by involving each one to the greatest extent possible in the assessment process in order to encourage pupils to set their own realistic short- and long-term goals.

Pupils spend their day working in groups, pairs or individually on projects they have chosen; on the day of my visit, children were studying themes ranging from archaeology to a presentation on a local factory that produces generators. All pupils are free to use the telephone, conveniently placed at the front of the classroom, when they need information from an outside source. A modem is used regularly to communicate with schools in France with which the class produces a weekly newsletter. Two daily newspapers are delivered to the school everyday and pupils regularly bring in resources from home.

Several factors indicate that the teaching approach adopted at Crauthem has been successful. This class had been considered by previous teachers as being a "difficult" group presenting a number of behavioural problems - the class teacher expresses no such difficulties. On the morning of my observation it was apparent that every pupil set about his self-appointed task autonomously and enthusiastically. Another yardstick to measure scholastic progress against that obtained by more traditional methods is provided by the national test that every child in Luxembourg must pass at the end of the primary cursus. In past years, Mr Fiermonte's class has attained the same overall level as counterparts in other schools throughout the country, yet he maintains that he does very little "formal teaching" in a year. How then do his pupils manage to cover the required curriculum? He considers that this is because children naturally seek certain knowledge at a certain age, the school curriculum to a large extent does no more than formalise a natural progression. Perhaps we should also take into account the fact that, because the teacher has freed himself from other tasks to concentrate on individualised teaching, pupils are benefiting from as much if not more pure teaching time than pupils taught in group. A second important element is timing: when children encounter a problem they cannot resolve with their peers, they are highly motivated and psychologically ready to receive and immediately apply the information the teacher will impart to them.

The class teacher considers that his style of teaching has not changed with the introduction of IT, but that new technology has opened up vast communication possibilities, facilitated many menial and time-consuming tasks, and increased pupil motivation, interaction and independence. His approach appears to have opened up new horizons in the following areas:

- **socialisation:** although pupils work individually, in pairs or in small groups, the computer screen immediately renders their work "public", other class members feel free to comment on what they see on-screen, thus developing co-operation, collaboration and a greater pride in work that can be seen by all
- **openness to the community:** easy access to outside sources of information has broken down the barrier between school and the outside world
- **openness to the world:** the production of a weekly newsletter has developed the pupils' capacity to see what news is important to, and can be shared with, others. Children take a more critical, personal and objective approach to what they read in the newspaper; it has also developed a more meaningful interest in geographical, demographic and cultural features of other parts of Europe, and a greater tolerance and understanding of other nationalities and ways of life
- **openness to the economic sector:** work on projects about the local economic sector has created a deeper understanding of the community, the responsibility of the individual in it and the need for professional skills to serve it.

Although the pupils observed at Crauthem are 11-12 year olds, this model could certainly be adapted to younger age groups. The success of this particular learning situation seems due to the philosophical approach rather than the training of the class teacher, though it should also be mentioned that he is an active member of a local association (APTICE, described in chapter 8) created

On-site Observation
GRID N° 7

SCHOOL/CLASS:	Mem Martins - Portugal - 6-12 yr olds
DATE:	08/05/1996
RELEVANCE OF IT:	A global approach to give children practice in IT in all areas
PROGRAM USED:	LOGO, DR HALO, FIRST PUBLISHER, in Windows environment. No task-specific programmes are commercially available in Portuguese
COMPUTER DISTRIBUTION:	4 computers in a Resource Centre linked to a telematic network. The centre is used alternately by 4 classes, each one day per week. 12 yr-olds use computer every day
INTERACTION ALLOWED BY SOFTWARE:	Children work individually, but are encouraged to help each other, exchange ideas, present different points of view. Computer work is seen as an occasion for socialisation
VARIETY OF ACTIVITIES TAKING PLACE SIMULTANEOUSLY:	Children work on individual projects, reply to diagnosis-incorporated worksheets or make their own worksheets. An entry prepared by one group in this class for a European day competition recently won first prize
TEACHER PURPOSE (3 CULTURES):	A cross-curricular approach
GROUP WORK/TEAM SPIRIT:	A noticeable improvement in most pupils in terms of self-esteem, team spirit, co-operation and integration
SENSE OF RESPONSIBILITY/ PERSONAL DISCIPLINE:	Many pupils show a great sense of responsibility and discipline; they show great independence in managing their time and their own activities on the computer
DEGREE OF DECISION-MAKING/COMMITMENT/WILLINGNESS TO TAKE RISKS:	Computer work has enabled chn to develop a sense of independence. One class of 12 yr-olds have produced their own book on literature
SENSE OF INITIATIVE/ CURIOSITY/CREATIVITY:	A marked improvement has been noted throughout the year in these three areas (e.g. the entry in the European day competition).
DEGREE OF ATOMISATION/ SOCIALISATION:	Chn have to be inventive since few programs are available Chn help each other, have learnt to accept and give constructive criticism. Far greater socialisation since "computer work" began
SENSE OF ACHIEVEMENT/ PRIDE IN WORK:	Rightly proud of their productions, chn work independently to complete their chosen projects
CORRESPONDENCE TO PURPOSE/LEVEL OF ACHIEVEMENT IN CULTURE:	The objective to introduce greater dynamism in classwork through use of IT has been achieved

Background grid page 143.

by teachers to exchange ideas on classroom use of IT and to arouse national awareness of the importance of this new tool in education.

A similar global approach recently discovered through the Instituto de Inovaçao Educacional in Portugal also merits closer examination. This class does not possess its own computer equipment, but for one full day per week moves into the resource centre for a project day. To make up for the lack of software in Portuguese, teachers supplement their general-purpose software with home-made worksheets that they exchange on a regular basis. Children choose their own cross-curricular activities and even make their own worksheets. Earlier this year, the originality and creativity of one group was rewarded with the first prize in a European Day competition organised through a telematics link.

Artistic expression

We cannot conclude a section dealing with expression and communication without also examining the impact of IT in artistic expression. Software in this range extends from simple paint and draw programs to music studios that offer budding musicians a full orchestra with which they can test and develop talents. Today even virtual cinematographic studios exist on CD-ROM, putting at the disposition of young artists a multitude of sound, images, ideas and special effects that will let them become "virtual" movie producers. Learners can develop their design and construction skills with building kits linked to LOGO programs (discussed in the previous section) which enable them to create their own models that can move and function. IT has greatly extended the creative possibilities that a teacher can offer his class, by deepening and widening the learner's experience and giving him greater access to creativity. The use of IT in artistic expression is also a convincing way of reconciling with technology not only the more artistic children who are often frustrated by the down-to-earth requirements of traditional learning methods, but also many girls who, through a traditional upbringing, are led to believe that IT is a strictly masculine domain that is not for them[24].

Creativity plays an important role in developing formal operational reasoning strategies, as it is yet another means by which the learner can express his vision of the world, and a particularly important one for children who have trouble expressing themselves through written or oral language. IT provides the learner with "professional-type" tools that are easy for young hands to manipulate and that will enhance the overall appearance of production, thereby developing greater confidence in the learner. The icons used to unlock the possibilities offered by programs act as an invitation for learners to explore. At the same time, they initiate learners to the language of symbols, a language that

24. Papert S., *The Children's Machine: Rethinking School in the Age of the Computer*, New York, Harvester/Wheatsheaf, 1993, p. 148-150

will serve them throughout their lives in widely diverse domains from reading a map and interpreting graphs and legends to finding their way in an unknown environment. IT frees the learner from repetitive tasks and, by giving access to pre-set colour, shape, texture, pattern and sound, enables him to focus on one skill area at a time. The templates and structures that are provided in most draw and paint packages encourage exploration of space and shape. Motivation remains high throughout the creative act, as IT shortens the time-gap between imagination and realisation. Boldness and risk-taking are encouraged because the learner feels more comfortable in a learning environment that allows privacy, is non-judgmental, gives total ownership (the learner is free to preserve or destroy) and provides unlimited resources (fresh starts, a new canvas at a stroke). IT allows for whole tasks to be divided into manageable chunks, when time runs out or tiredness sets in the work can be saved on a disk that can also be used to record a pupil's consecutive creations and later serve both teacher and learner as a means of assessing progress[25].

Software for musical expression opens up a whole new world that to date remains relatively unexploited in the school environment. It invites children into a musical environment in which they can acquaint themselves with the sound produced by each individual instrument of a full orchestra, even change instruments in popular tunes on pre-recorded sound tracks if they wish, and watch the music playing on a musical score that highlights each note as it is played. Without IT, opportunities for primary school children to work with sheet music are usually reserved for the elite few who can afford private music lessons; even children who are lucky enough to be taken to concerts will rarely have the opportunity to listen to the sound of orchestral instruments separately. In musical expression programs, pupils can choose their own instrument (each one is attributed a colour) to try their hand at composing music, using a mouse to guide the note of their choice across the scale until they hear the sound they wish. With a click of the mouse, the learner poses his notes one at a time on the score sheet to complete his composition. One by one, extra instruments can be added to achieve the sound effect desired. Or music can be composed through use of forms and colour, each colour representing a different instrument, each movement being linked by pitch and by rhythm to a series of notes.

We are certainly not suggesting that IT can replace music teachers. On the contrary, musical programs of this type provide an incentive for children to want to learn music by allowing them to design tasks and resolve problems in an environment that reflects the way knowledge can be used once it has been acquired[26].

---

25. Hart B., Holt G., Fletcher C., Tyldesley A., *Extending Horizons,* U.K., NCET, 1994, Imaginations in the Making
26. Delacôte G., *Savoir apprendre: les nouvelles méthodes,* Paris, Editions Odile Jacob, 1996, p.157-158

Data-logging and information handling

In primary grades, data-logging and information handling are essentially skills used in the area of natural science. Perhaps then we should take a closer look at the aims of natural science in the curriculum. In most countries, the emphasis has moved away from "content" to be replaced by learning through action. The objective is to lead the child to discover the complex world around him and develop his own "scientific method" through observation, recording, planning, designing tasks, comparison, contrast, classification, analysis, interpreting, detecting patterns and trends, formulation and testing of hypotheses, verbalisation of findings, conceptualisation and self-regulation (i.e. modifying, correcting or adding to concepts formed through past experience to create new concepts and hence progress in the learning spiral). When a child is given opportunities to form new concepts about his environment he will, in the long term, have greater control over it.

The processes of data-logging and information handling can be greatly enhanced by the use of general purpose software programs such as spreadsheets, graph plotters and data-bases, which enable pupils to gather and store much more information faster than was previously possible with pencil and paper methods[27]. Such software facilitates and streamlines the tasks of manipulation, interrogation and interpretation as it can be used to present data in a form that will bring out the significance of results and make patterns and trends more accessible. Automatic computation options save time and will overcome any interpretation errors due to mathematical mistakes when pupils are investigating results. Graph facilities in spreadsheet programs enable pupils to present their work in attractive and meaningful ways unavailable without the help of the computer. Observations become more pertinent because of the greater mass of data that can be collected and because of alternative classification possibilities that can be carried out by the computer. And once again, prompt feedback and interaction between children make the learning experience one of collaboration and communication[28].

The use of more sophisticated computer programs or input devices can also extend the range of observable phenomena and increase the physical quality of data measurement, though we shall not discuss such IT applications here as they are usually only accessible to secondary schools or universities.

"Getting Started with Information Handling"

General-purpose software can be used with pupils at a very early age to introduce them to the skills of data handling and logging. Most of the activities

---

27. NCET, *Getting started with Information Handling*, U.K., NCET, 1994
28. Group report, A Role for Information Technology in Practical Science, in the Final Report of the 45th European Teachers' Seminar, *Information Technology in Science Education*, Council of Europe, 1989, p. 57-59.

included in the natural science curriculum for 8-to-10 year olds are concerned with collecting information from the immediate environment. Spreadsheets with graph facilities provide an easy means for young children to record this data, over time if necessary, and can be used to produce exciting visual supports that help children retain facts learned. A perfect example of this is a year-long project on weather to improve children's understanding of seasons. A thermometer can be used to measure temperature and a container to collect rainfall over regular 24-hour periods. By storing information on a spreadsheet children can progressively plot two line graphs which will highlight the relationship between temperature and precipitation and illustrate weather trends as the seasons change. This same method can be applied to plot the growth of the children themselves over the school year, to measure growth in plants in different environments (warmer, wetter, etc.), to measure the amount of insect-life in different soil types or the effects of various types of clothing to retain heat[29].

The NCET has put out an excellent kit "Getting Started with Information Handling", especially adapted for use in the early years of primary education. This kit includes floppy disks for use on Apple, Archimedes or P.C. that can be read directly into an application such as Excel, but also informs the teacher of all existing IT applications that could be used with children of this age to develop information handling skills across the curriculum. The booklet and information sheets included with the disks clearly set out lesson plans which will give children the opportunity to:

- identify a purpose/raise key questions
- plan, hypothesise, predict
- identify the most appropriate software tool for the task
- design and carry out an investigation
- identify patterns and relationships
- develop analytical skills
- present and communicate ideas
- evaluate and refine investigation

This pedagogical package is presented in such a way that even the most computer-illiterate teacher is tempted to use the computer in class. Advice is given on lesson planning and all the technological aspects, from selection of software to organisation and position of hardware, pre- and post-computer work organisation, and time needed for children to progress to analysing, interpreting and presenting findings. Moreover, the booklet explains in detail the process of assessment, not only in terms of individual results but more importantly the intellectual process followed by each child and the level of pupil interaction achieved.

---

29. NCET, *Primary Science Investigations with IT*, UK, NCET, 1994.

Information handling and data-logging activities provide an ideal opportunity for children to work in groups around the computer, and hence favour pupil-to-pupil/pupil-to-knowledge interactions. Pupils work together to plan, hypothesise and predict, then simulate their predictions to affirm or reformulate their hypothesis.

An information handling project via an electronic link

*This project concerns a British class of severely handicapped learners who came to discover their environment through an exchange that began with an e-mail link set up with a class of children living in Norway. It was inspired by a subject included in the geography program of the national curriculum, the object of which was to study and compare the local environment of the school with a contrasting location in another country. The project could never have taken place or had such far-reaching effects without the contribution of Information Technology.

All of the nine 14-18 year-olds in the class suffer from severe learning disabilities including severe difficulties with communication, literacy, numeracy, social skills and personal perception (low levels of self esteem). The special school these pupils attend had recently relocated onto an island and the Norwegian island of Rovaer was chosen so that the pupils could undertake a comparative study of the two islands. To do so the pupils had to work as a team to consider, compile and agree to a list of questions which was then to be communicated to their project partners. This they did by using symbol-to-word software[30], a valuable communication tool for children locked in a world of silence through physical handicaps or learning impairments. With symbol-to-word software the traditional keyboard is covered by an overlay keyboard with symbols replacing the letters. To enter the words they wish to express, the children type in the symbols. The software "reads" the text to the pupils as they enter it on the keyboard, automatically converting the symbols to the words that will be sent through e-mail. The pupils keep their own copy of the e-mail in both words and symbols.

It was not long before the exchange necessitated the services of "snail mail" as the UK school explored their island and compiled a package of maps, leaflets and photographs. The Rovaer Skole reciprocated. In fact, the two schools had already worked together a year or so earlier on a project on the Vikings, but in this new project postage stamps were exchanged for the first time. The remarkable point is: at no stage in the communication did the Rovaer Skole pupils realise that they were communicating with children any different from themselves. Information technology was providing a cloak of anonymity and in

* Thanks are extended to the staff of Imagination Technology for the information recorded on this project.
30. Hart B., Holt G., Fletcher C., Tyldesley A., *Extending Horizons*, U.K., NCET, 1994, Using symbols to enhance English

A SAMPLE OF SYMBOL-TO-WORD PRODUCTION

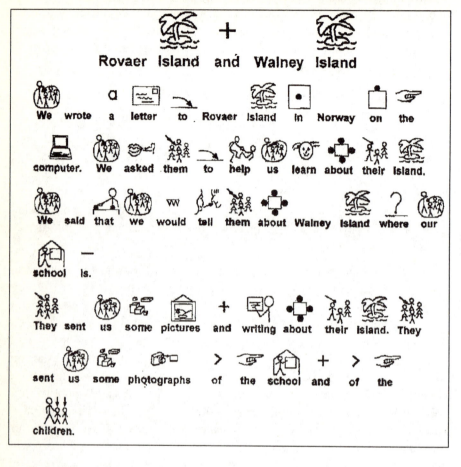

the process widening the pupils' awareness of the world in which they live, improving the geographical vocabulary of some of the children and leading them to use maps for comparison and interpretation. Some children increased their understanding of the economic activity which sustained the area in which they lived, in contrast to a very small island off the coast of Norway.

Bob Hart from Imagination Technology, an organisation which specialises in organising and assessing IT activities for special needs pupils, reports on the learning gains resulting from this project: "The activity had a very positive influence on the self esteem of this group of pupils. It increased their confidence and enhanced their language development. It provided access to powerful technology which in itself conveys messages about being valued members of society and offers opportunities for equality. It served to awaken curiosity in pupils who seldom question the world about them. The activity also resulted in some interesting displays of work on the classroom walls. This in turn brought positive comments from visitors and this further increased the positive perceptions of what the pupils could achieve. The overall project also had an effect on the adults working with the pupils; they too were drawn into the learning process as it created a culture in which all were learners."

This is a remarkable example of a project that started out simply as a means of developing a greater awareness of the environment in pupils through information handling and the comparison and exchange of data.

Chapter 5

IT as a source of reference

Given the enormous amount of data that can be stored on a CD-ROM, this medium is obviously rapidly replacing books and encyclopaedias in many school libraries. The CD-ROM offers children easy access to a wealth of information in sound, text and moving images, not only giving added reality to events that children would have difficulty in experiencing elsewhere but also putting information into a factual context that can be printed out and used in project work. Searching, accessing and retrieving information poses an exciting challenge for classroom practice[31] since the richness of an overall experience is necessarily related to purpose-driven exploration. Several projects carried out in this domain merit further investigation.

"Living books"

A *Living book* is a CD-ROM presentation of a children's story in picture "pages" with sound-enhanced moving pop-ups and texts, narration and dialogues telling the story. Each new page begins with an animation, then the image freezes and each word of the text is highlighted as it is "read", in much the same way as teachers lead children to "read" nursery rhymes printed on the board as a means of familiarising pre-readers with the shape of words. Once the page has been read, the child can explore the image by clicking on different parts with a mouse to activate pop-ups and sounds. Such books are an attractive and playful way of introducing younger children (at pre-reading and early reading levels) to the pleasure of "reading", particularly for children who have not yet discovered the joy of being read to in the home environment. Teachers of infant classes in the United Kingdom where this form of IT is being used report that *Living books* are proving especially valuable in motivating young pupils to develop active listening skills. The variety of voices and accents seem to have improved their ability to infer and read between the lines.

The obvious difficulty with any computer work at this age-level is that it must be used either as a whole class activity, thereby greatly limiting the number of children "actively" exploring the image pop-ups through use of the mouse, or, for teachers lucky enough to have several computers at their

---

31. Daly F., *CD-ROM in Education*, U.K., NCET, 1995, p.4.

disposition, as a group activity, but in this case the class relies heavily on the volunteer efforts of available parents. Few schools are fortunate enough to have an adequate supply of computers and volunteer workers. A number of titles exist in this series, which unfortunately have not yet found their way onto the lending shelves of local libraries.

The CD-ROM as a source of learning and reference material

In 1994, the NCET implemented a project in the United Kingdom designed to assess the value of CD-ROMs in primary education, both as a means of catering to the wide range of pupil abilities to be found in any one class and of providing ready resource material for non-specialist primary teachers. All participating schools, today a total of 5,000, were equipped with a multimedia platform and 6 CD-ROM titles. 24% of schools had bought more titles within one year after the start up of their project.

Before launching the project, the NCET assessed performances of 20 hardware systems and over 500 CD-ROM titles and sent out a field officer to all schools concerned to develop the support material that would help teachers integrate the material into their program of work. Preparations before implementation got underway also included a training course intended to show all teachers receiving computers how to use them for their personal work (to gain the necessary confidence to introduce IT in class), and to make them aware of the numerous possibilities that multimedia offers. *The catalogue published as a result of CD assessment (now updated annually) is a most useful document that informs teachers not only of content, but also of age-suitability and curriculum relevance. The teachers encountered during our visit would like to see included in the catalogue an overview chart of the content of each title, enabling them to make a more enlightened choice when seeking material that will fit into their teaching program. They feel that each title should be accompanied by worksheet resources in order to facilitate their choice of supplementary (hard-copy) resources to be made available to children before and after their multimedia session.

In the class observed, children work in pairs throughout the day for half hour sessions in a room adjoining the classroom, whilst the teacher continues normal class work with the remaining pupils. The subject under study on the day of my visit was "Musical Instruments". These are presented on the CD-ROM by country (on a colourful world map emphasising the differences and similarities of musical cultures), by type (wind, percussion, etc.), by name and by sound. Enthusiasm remained high throughout the session, as the children were working on quiz sheets in competition with other groups. Nevertheless, several of the pupils were a little disgruntled in having to use quiz sheets which "... take up too

---

* Daly F., *CD-ROM in Education*, U.K., NCET, 1995

On-site Observation
GRID N° 8

SCHOOL/CLASS:	Leicestershire Little Hill Primary School - UK
DATE:	07/06/1995
RELEVANCE OF IT:	Use of CD-ROM to enable 8-10 year-olds to discover musical instruments
PROGRAM USED:	Musical Instruments (page 383, CD-ROM in Education, NCET)
COMPUTER DISTRIBUTION:	Computer placed in a room adjoining classroom, children work at computers in pairs for 1/2 hour sessions throughout day whilst teacher continues normal work with rest of class
INTERACTION ALLOWED BY SOFTWARE:	High degree of interaction around computer, interaction with rest of class to discuss findings when all have completed their quiz
VARIETY OF ACTIVITIES TAKING PLACE SIMULTANEOUSLY:	Children at computer are searching, matching, discussing & discovering use of CD-ROM as a resource, teacher's quiz provides a goal and direction in their activities
TEACHER PURPOSE (3 CULTURES):	Humanities: to familiarise children with musical culture & to evoke curiosity about instruments from other countries (national instruments can be accessed by choosing a country on the map)
GROUP WORK/TEAM SPIRIT:	The two pairs of children observed cooperate enthusiastically, discussing decisions before taking action. A high degree of competition evident between teams
SENSE OF RESPONSIBILITY/ PERSONAL DISCIPLINE:	All chat is task-oriented & no adult supervision necessary, though children insist they would rather have time to discover instruments of their choice without having to complete the teacher's quiz
DEGREE OF DECISION-MAKING/COMMITMENT/WILL INGNESS TO TAKE RISKS:	A high level of decision-making is involved because 4 means of instrument selection are available, children generally discuss their path of action
SENSE OF INITIATIVE/ CURIOSITY/CREATIVITY:	They listen to most sound samples, often taking the initiative to go back to hear similar instruments. They choose their own order of tackling questions as a means of having more time to "listen"
DEGREE OF ATOMISATION/ SOCIALISATION:	High degree of socialisation in pairs since they have to make decisions as to the best path to take, which music to listen to, etc. Pupils choose their partner, but often change partners according to who is ready when their turn comes
SENSE OF ACHIEVEMENT/ PRIDE IN WORK:	Children are eager to complete their task and carefully choose which parts to print out to present with their quiz
CORRESPONDENCE TO PURPOSE/LEVEL OF ACHIEVEMENT IN CULTURE:	The task corresponds to the objective, i.e. the children discover new instruments, learn which family they belong to, discover similarities between cultures and are introduced to new sounds

Background grid page 144.

much time, we can't explore everything that is on the CD-ROM". With four paths available for instrument selection, animated conversations often arose as to which path would be the most appropriate to obtain the knowledge required to fill in the quiz sheet. It was amusing to see that each pair of pupils had, from previous multimedia sessions, devised their own shortcuts to tackle the questions as rapidly as possible (disregarding the order on the sheet and regrouping in terms of where the answer should be found), leaving themselves time to go back and listen again to the instruments they found the most intriguing. A second important decision that led to concerted negotiation was the choice of which texts and images should be printed out to enhance the presentation of their findings.

No formal assessment has yet been made of learning gains from this project but, from the great enthusiasm of learners, it is evident that children find CD-ROMs a challenge in terms of resolving the problem of how to reach the information they have set out to find, and an exciting universe in sound, text, images and motion that can be explored dozens of times - there is always something new to discover.

"Libraries of the Future"

Libraries of the Future is a UK project designed to test the use of electronic information resources (Internet, CD-ROM, etc.) in the teaching and learning process. In the framework of this concept, a pilot scheme was set up in a total 270 educational establishments, including 20 primary and secondary schools, to trial the joint BBC/NCET *Auntielink* intended to assess and develop electronic communication applications suitable for use in schools. Internet has far-reaching implications in education, firstly for the fantastically rich reserve of information on a wide range of subjects that it puts at the disposition of learners and, secondly, because it brings the outside "adult" world into the classroom. In the primary school, it provides a means of encouraging pupils to learn independently and enhances the development of cross-curricular skills such as information retrieval, handling and presentation. The pupils encountered at a participating school in the UK were fully aware of their privilege to be involved in the project and thrilled at the fact that "you can learn anything, a book only gives you information about one thing". Teachers involved in the project are delighted with the extent to which their relationship with pupils has been enriched, now that they "are learning together with their pupils on an equal footing". Volunteer parents are once again largely involved in helping out teachers with the extra assistance and supervision needed in work involving small groups.

One interesting aspect observed in the use of Internet is that, because there is just one connected computer for a whole class, "scouts" must be chosen at each

On-site Observation
GRID N° 9

SCHOOL/CLASS:	Potters Green Primary School -UK - KS2 (9 yr-olds)
DATE:	06/06/1995
RELEVANCE OF IT:	Use of Internet to find out about Finland, in conjunction with class project on food
PROGRAM USED:	BBC/NC Auntielink
COMPUTER DISTRIBUTION:	5 children working together on computer in corner of classroom in which tchr is working with rest of class. A "helping" mother works with group
INTERACTION ALLOWED BY SOFTWARE:	Chn are totally absorbed in their task, gathering information (which they must then share with class) depends not only on asking right question, but also formulating it correctly
VARIETY OF ACTIVITIES TAKING PLACE SIMULTANEOUSLY:	Exploration by enquiry, group negotiation as to what & how to ask, peer-correction on errors, formulation/verification of hypotheses, scanning for information
TEACHER PURPOSE (3 CULTURES):	Exploration in social sciences, reading for information, relating information to class
GROUP WORK/TEAM SPIRIT:	Chn are excited about their task, collaborate to find best solution, learn to accept peer-correction
SENSE OF RESPONSIBILITY/ PERSONAL DISCIPLINE:	No behavioural problems since chn are fully concentrated on task, finding best bits to print out for class. Show drive in trying to work out best way to satisfy needs when confronted with a mass of information
DEGREE OF DECISION-MAKING/COMMITMENT/WILL INGNESS TO TAKE RISKS:	High; computer doesn't always "understand", but they know that the information is there somewhere, continuously making new enquiry decisions
SENSE OF INITIATIVE/ CURIOSITY/CREATIVITY:	Curiosity is awakened by many details found en-route, initiative & creativity in question formulation and association-building
DEGREE OF ATOMISATION/ SOCIALISATION:	Chn working as a nuclear group to scout for information to share with class; socialisation around computer is high. Class collaborates by "sending" their questions to today's exploration group
SENSE OF ACHIEVEMENT/ PRIDE IN WORK:	High when they manage to find something really appropriate, print outs are presented with pride
CORRESPONDENCE TO PURPOSE/LEVEL OF ACHIEVEMENT IN CULTURE:	Provides an ideal means of exploring outside world for appropriate & meaningful information, considerable gains in reading skills have been noted

Background grid page 145.

session to go out and retrieve the information that the whole class has decided necessary, then report back to the class with the fruit of their research. With such a heavy weight of responsibility on their shoulders, young learners spend a remarkable amount of energy during and between lessons to devise the most efficient routes that can be taken in their quest. Questions must be expressed concisely and clearly, alternatives must be quickly formulated if a first attempt is not fruitful. Here the volunteer "supervisor" takes on an important role in assisting the children with sometimes unfamiliar terms. Teachers, children and volunteers alike have received no formal training, self-help and "cascade" models seem to be the most prevalent for all involved.

The NCET "Libraries of the future" project report lists a number of learning gains in language and communication that can be directly attributed to use of Internet/CD-ROM:

- improvements in reading and writing, pupils want to read better with greater understanding,
- learners have fewer spelling-related difficulties when looking up topics on CD-ROM,
- language skills have improved through discussion of the steps of the tasks they have been working on and, perhaps more importantly, because they have become motivated to watch and discuss television news programmes with their parents at home,
- information has become a more personal thing for pupils, and their interest in world and current affairs has been stimulated by use and manipulation of CD-ROM and Internet.

Internet is being used in relatively few European classrooms to date, mainly because of high telephone costs, lack of telephones available in classrooms and libraries and, more particularly, the dangers of access to unauthorised programs (see chapter 7).

A lending library on disk*

The Comenius project in the Netherlands has already started making provision to train young pupils in how to use real-life "Libraries of the future". One of the programs available with the Comenius starter package - *DOCO-Vista* - is used to computerise schools' documentation and media centres, as well as the reading library, the teachers' library and the remedial library if the school wishes. From the age of 8 onwards, children can use a computer to look for their own reference material under keyword, title, author, series, placement number or reading level. Obviously, at first young pupils will need assistance from the librarian or volunteer parents who help out in the library, but once they are

---

* Thanks are extended to the staff of PRINT, NL, for the information provided on DOCO.

capable of working at the computer independently or in pairs they are encouraged to manage their own library activities with little intervention from an adult.

The program also includes a lending function that children use when they borrow a book, and a registration function that enables the teacher or librarian to monitor and evaluate the lending and research procedure. Children can be entered with attached indications e.g. reading skills, which then makes it possible to block all material that would be too difficult for them. It is also possible to enter reading levels, thereby limiting access to documentation that would be below the stipulated levels. A label can also be given to materials, to avoid pupils being confronted with material that is not suitable for them.

At present, the input of material must be done for each school individually, but in the future data on all material described in education reviews and included in the supply list will be available on disk. Schools that use administration packages such as *SIS* (discussed in chapter 8) can automatically transfer data on pupils to *DOCO*.

It is reassuring to see that, at least in the Netherlands, primary school libraries are beginning to develop information retrieval and handling strategies in an environment that resembles the reality that learners often encounter for the first time when they reach university level.

*

*   *

Of course, a great many teachers who are deprived of the opportunity to use IT in class activities because of lack of material are already using the computer in diverse ways to enrich and enhance the work that is carried out in class: word-processing and graphics to prepare worksheets and teaching aids, databases and spreadsheets to monitor pupils' progress, electronic network resources to download text and images for use in classroom, electronic communication links to gather information on training and resources available...

Chapter 6

Providing equal learning opportunities

As we have seen in the previous chapters, IT can help to overcome a great number of learning difficulties and enable even the most severely physically handicapped children to develop the autonomy necessary to access information and knowledge. New IT applications are continually being developed in an effort to ensure that a maximum number of children can complete their basic education in mainstream primary school establishments. Both Germany and the Netherlands have defined in their national primary education policy the objective to reduce by 50% the number of children sent to special schools. But learning impairments and physical handicaps are not the only obstacles today's generation must overcome if they are to become fully-fledged citizens and play an active role in democracy.

The fracture in the social fabric of our nations, shall we say in all the nations of the world, is today a reality. Unemployment, political dissension, economic uncertainty, civil war and military combats between neighbouring countries are all a reflection of this fracture. Over two centuries ago, Jean-Jacques Rousseau sent out his message of alert: "Discord and moral confusion are the ineluctable consequences of excessive inequalities of wealth and of the size and complexity of modern society; only self-knowledge and self-mastery can bring happiness and social harmony. Man cannot be happy and free, cannot be on good terms with himself and his neighbours except in a community simple enough to enable him to take a full and equal part in its government.... Men cannot be truly free unless they are emotionally secure, which they will be only in a society of equals, where each man depends, not on the caprice or protection of some person or group stronger or wealthier than himself, but on a system of laws which are the same for all men and are made by the entire community"[32].

It is the role of primary education[33] to help create this "society of equals", to allow each and every child to develop self-knowledge and self-mastery by providing equal opportunities for all children to become autonomous lifelong learners capable of accessing information and reasoning in ways that will permit them to exercise their rights to take a full and equal part in our

32. Rousseau, J-J., *Du Contrat Social*, extract from the Encyclopaedia Brittanica
33. Council for Cultural Co-operation: School Education Division, *Innovation in Primary Education*, Strasbourg, Council of Europe, 1988, p.7

governments. To do so it must overcome, to the greatest extent possible, not only the obstacles of physical handicaps and learning impairments, but also those created by insufficiently developed reasoning capacity, socio-economic factors[34] and even by the transmission of traditional roles that often make it more difficult for girls to have access to technology than boys (cf. Children of the Future project).

Computer "games" to overcome language learning impairments

Literacy is a subject that is often in the news nowadays. In May, 1996, French national television newscasters broke the alarming news that 25% of children in the first year of high school (11 to 12 years) were unable to read and write sufficiently to commence high school studies. This figure is surprisingly close to those disclosed in 1983 by the Academy of Nice in France: 22% of the pupils who enter secondary education cannot read, 45% are incapable of executing a definite instruction conveyed by a written order and 72% are unable to comprehend the sense of one word from its context[35].

One of the contributing factors to illiteracy is language learning impairment[36]. A group of scientists at the Center for Molecular and Behavioural Neuroscience at Rutgers University in Newark, New Jersey, recently carried out a study on children suffering from language learning impairment stemming from an inability to decode spoken words. Results suggest that the use of adapted computer "games" (in fact, carefully devised drills based on auditory discrimination strategies) may dramatically develop auditory skills in children.

The children enrolled in the Rutgers study all had difficulty distinguishing among phonemes (the basic building blocks of language), "not because they cannot hear the sounds, but because the auditory centres of the brain can't process them" (Tallal P.). Researchers at Rutgers, working in collaboration with researchers at the University of California at San Francisco, found that when children are taught to distinguish sounds that have been slowed down and exaggerated, they learn to distinguish between these sounds in ordinary speech. To reinforce this training, scientists developed computer games in which children learn to distinguish between phonemes and are rewarded when then do so by lively animations. As a child's performance improves, the exaggeration of the sounds is decreased. The report indicates that out of a total twenty two children who took part in the experimental program that began last summer (1995) at Rutgers, the performance level of several of the children had jumped

---

34. Plaisance E., Vergnaud G., *Les sciences de l'education*, Paris, La découverte, 1993, p. 60

35. de Landsheere G., *L'illetrisme, une menace pour les individus et l'économie du pays*, to be published

36 This section is entirely based on: Merzenich MM, Jenkins WM, Johnston P, Schreiner C, Miller SL, Tallal P,: Temporal processing deficits of language-learning impaired children ameliorated by training, in *Science*, USA, 5th Jan. 1996, N° 271, p.77 - 81;

Nash J.M., Zooming in on Dyslexia, in *Time International*, 26th January, 1996, P. 38-40

by as much as two years after just four weeks of therapy, at a rhythm of three hours per day, five days a week. Researchers believe that this same language-processing "glitch" may be the root of the more common problem of dyslexia, a reading disability that affects perhaps more than 15% of the American population. Experts in Europe place this figure closer to 10%.*

Although no study similar to that carried out by Tallal et al. is yet underway in Europe, this type of application could represent a means of providing equal learning opportunities to children who are inevitably left behind at an early age because of language learning impairment.

Overcoming handicaps created by socio-economic environment

In Sweden an interesting study was carried out to examine the effects of IT as a means of offering equal learning opportunities to children from widely varying socio-professional categories.

Children of the Future[37] is a three-year-long Research and Development project carried out in Leisure Centres - a government run institution for child care out of school hours. The study concerns 13 centres (some of them located up to 1,000 km apart) with about 15 children per centre (ages ranging from 7 - 12 years); 75% of the children involved in the project are 7 - 9 years old. Each centre is equipped with one computer complete with hard disk, printer, software and modem. During the project, children work together with computers to produce newspapers and databases. They work with word processing, graphics, database and desk-top publishing programs and electronic mail. The centres have no "educational software", software products especially designed for children or computer games. As the point of departure was that the activity should be able to function at any ordinary centre, the staff was given just one day of training before the start of the program, then two more days three weeks later. All educators attend a two-day seminar every term, where they discuss with the project leader the aims, plans, evaluation and results for the period.

The project is being conducted by Tommy Isaksson, Lecturer at the University College of Falun/Borlänge, who clearly explains the motivation behind the study, "As a College of Education lecturer in social sciences, teaching pre-school teachers, recreation instructors and primary school teachers, I have observed that knowledge of and insight into society, its changes and its influence on our departments of education are of great importance as a means of creating a teaching environment preparing children and young people for the

---

* Precise figures are not available, this is an estimate made by the French association, APEDA, created by parents to help children with severe reading difficulties.

37. This section is almost entirely based upon an as yet unpublished report: Isaksson T., *Children of the Future*, Sweden, 1995

"real world"."... " Computerisation reinforces the prevailing structure of society - this means that an undemocratic system becomes more undemocratic with computerised routines and a democratic system becomes - or has the necessary requirements for becoming - more democratic."

This, however, is subject to one condition: that each and every citizen acquire a mode of inductive and deductive reasoning that will allow him to develop his capacity of discernment and decision in regards to knowledge; it is only in this way that the citizen can maintain, even augment, his own degree of liberty, and hence the degree of democracy prevalent in the society. If our educational system does not succeed in transmitting this potential to each citizen, an elite class increasingly limited in demographic terms will collectively and unconsciously monopolise the decision-making process, to the detriment of democracy.

The following tables, drawn from a preliminary study carried out at the beginning of the Swedish project and based on a 6-level socio-economic classification scale used throughout to record data, highlights the inequality that exists between boys and girls, and children from middle and upper social classes as compared to those from "lower" socio-professional levels in terms of having a computer at home on which they can work and play. We can suppose that these figures are reasonably representative of other European countries.

A COMPUTER AT HOME, SOCIAL CLASS AND GENDER

	Workers employees	Non-manual	Professionals self-employed	Sum
Access	19.4%	20.9%	48.4%	25.3%
No access	80.6%	79.1%	51.6%	74.7%
	Lower social classes		Upper social classes	
Access	21.2%		30.1%	
No access	78.8%		69.9%	
	"Lower" boys	"Upper" boys	"Lower" girls	"Upper" girls
Access	35.4%	31.7%	8.2%	28.1%
No access	64.6%	68.3%	91.8%	71.9%

Source: report by Isaksson T., Children of the Future, 1995

It is even more interesting to look at the responses children gave when asked: "Who is the owner of the computer you use to work and play?"

COMPUTER OWNERSHIP AND GENDER			
	Boys	Girls	Sum
Myself	55.2%	0%	39%
Father	27.6%	58%	36.6%
Mother	3.5%	0%	2.4%
Brother	3.45%	16.7%	7.3%
Sister	0%	0%	0%
Relative	0%	8.3%	2.4%
"Everybody"	10.3%	16.7%	12.2%

Source: report by Isaksson T., Children of the Future, 1995

One of the central aims of *Children of the Future* is to promote equal opportunity between girls and boys, and also between children from all walks of life. The project is mainly intended, however, to develop an educational method for work with children and computers in the information society, to build an infrastructure between children and educators based on computer communication and electronic mail, to increase knowledge about the computer as an educational aid, and to develop children's social competence.

Data for the study is collected in two ways: at the beginning of the project, then again one year later, children fill out a questionnaire about computers, their interest in computers, etc. They also keep a journal recording work with computer, time spent, etc.

The children work together on the computers to produce newspapers and databases, using the immediate environment as a theme for their activities e.g. interviews and investigations in the area. The results are sent to all the other centres by electronic mail and compiled into a magazine. The children in each centre have also produced a database about their own interests, which was sent on to the 12 other centres to produce one big database. The children themselves consult the database to find new interests, new friends and pen-pals. Once a year all the children meet in a big "Children of the Future Festival" for two days during schooltime, somewhere in Sweden, where they can meet their computer friends and take part in social activities.

During one year, the mean average of project computer work per child is about 3 hours, plus 3 hours for free-time work. Children can thus be calculated as low or high users in project or free time. Not surprisingly, the data shows that although 34.7% of all children are free-time high users, only 22.2% are high users in project time, yet 27.3% of girls are high project-time users compared to only 17.7% for boys. Results also show that upper class children make the most of free-time opportunities, but lower class children and girls are at a disadvantage during free-time work. This can perhaps be explained by the fact that, because of the models they have seen in their immediate environment, lower class children have not had the opportunity to learn to construct their own activities. As has been mentioned several times in this study, girls are often hesitant in their approach to technology due to the role models that are transmitted from generation to generation, clearly evident when we look at the figures on computer ownership in the home.

After one year, comparison of results recorded on the questionnaires show that girls find computing less difficult than boys and, whereas 6% of "upper class" boys find computing less fun, interest has increased by 4% for boys of the unskilled/skilled worker category. More girls than boys want to use computers when they grow up.

The findings of this study illustrate how attitudes towards the computer can change if all children are given equal access opportunities, but also highlights some interesting points about differences between computer use for boys and girls. Girls in the study like to draw beautiful pictures and write careful stories whereas boys are keen to experiment more. This is a natural phenomenon - boys' and girls' brains do not function in exactly the same manner. Complementarity is an important element in all societies; all are equal in terms of value and service to the community. It is up to the education system to cater to, but certainly not thwart, the natural differences in rhythm and aptitude in pupils, by providing opportunities for learners to recognise and develop their potential for independent learning.

The survey is to be followed up by a series of interviews focusing on the causes of the girls' increased interest in information technology. Work is also continuing on the development of an educational method for work with children and computers in preparation for the information society. The project has already given 200 "Children of the Future" computer access, when most of the 600,000 children in Sweden aged between 7 and 12 have no access at all.

Chapter 7

A word of warning

Proceeding with precaution

In the last few chapters, readers have been given a glimpse of the enormous wealth of possibilities that are within the reach of our educational systems, if only teachers are given the chance to implement them. But no innovation is without its side-effects, so perhaps now it is time to examine more closely some of the factors that should be taken into consideration before charging headlong into the adventure of "Information Technology for all".

In a booklet published in 1985 by the Minister of Education and Cultural Affairs of North-Rhine-Westphalia, our attention is drawn to the fact that humanity does not yet clearly understand the dangers of the Information Age now underway. Only today is man beginning to suffer the long-term consequences brought about by intensive use of chemical products and the effects of pollution brought about through transformations in the types of energy used over the past century. At present it is impossible to hypothesise on the long-term effects of this new raw material - informatics - on the human mind. Communication structures are undergoing mutations because of a multiplication of communication possibilities and the demands of a media message which no longer takes place between individuals. The barrier between work and leisure has been broken down; firstly because of an enormous increase in computerised entertainment programs; secondly because work, shopping, banking, etc. can now be carried out at home. The family and the school therefore has new tasks to fulfil because of the necessity today for the citizen himself to learn to manage and harmonise work, leisure, educational and consumer activities.

In light of the above reflections, it is not surprising to discover that most of the 16 länders in Germany are still hesitating as to whether computers should be systematically introduced into the classroom. Thirty pilot projects are underway in North Rhine-Westphalia, a number of them concerned with telematic connections for educational purposes, and a decision should be made on national implementation policy in 1996. At present, computers in German primary schools are almost non-existent and information technology is not included in the teacher training curriculum.

The "rational" nature of man

Man has a great advantage in being able to use increasingly powerful tools to accomplish vast and complex tasks and to establish systematic interconnections. However, when we consider the inherent limitations of computer logic, and if we attempt to understand and simulate all domains of human thought, we should not lose sight of the danger that "instrumental" reasoning could become the predominant way of thinking and, in the process, banish to a large extent creativity, aestheticism and ethics from our thinking, as well as all that is not quantifiable in the domain of the irrational. Professional life could become dehumanised, creative and critical thinking relegated to the domain of leisure. To counteract these effects, the school must place great emphasis on developing creativity, aestheticism and critical thinking at an early age.

Although IT considerably increases the volume of information and experiences available to man, it reduces his opportunities to experience events directly and act autonomously. There is a great risk that information will become less transparent, and hence that man will have greater difficulty in determining whether the information that he is given is fact or fiction, real or virtual. This is perhaps one of the reasons why it has been noted throughout Europe that "alternative" educational establishments, those that believe in the natural method of letting pupils discover knowledge through their encounter with nature, are for the most part reluctant to introduce IT into their pedagogical approach. If we consider education in light of the new technology in information and communication that has invaded our lives, we can conclude that schools more than ever before need to offer real and concrete experiences. Will mediatic communication and the electronic processing of text, data and televised images tend to distance education even further from the realities of the natural world?[38] A child, by nature, lives in an imaginative world; if he does not learn to discriminate he will grow up in a world of virtual reality and not know where to draw the line between what is real and what is virtual.

Primary education has a major role to play if we are to avoid the pitfalls of the information age - today's pupils are tomorrow's citizens. Children need a thorough understanding of how IT functions, what objectives can be achieved and under which circumstances it should not be used. To answer to this challenge, teachers need not only knowledge and understanding of hardware and software, but also a deep philosophical understanding of the nature of the subject. Effective use of IT requires the development of new pedagogical skills and abilities related to class organisation, management and teaching style. Innovative teachers have always incorporated multimedia - literally, a mixture of media - in their lessons by means of the spoken word, recorded sounds,

---

38. This section is based on *Technologies nouvelles dans le domaine de l'information et communication à l'école - concept cadre*, Dusseldorf, Minister of Cultural Affairs of North-Westphalie Rheinland, 1985.

images and text. It is no secret to them that the average individual retains 10% of what he sees, 20% of what he hears, 50% of what he reads and 80% of what he sees, hears and does[39]. IT definitely facilitates the introduction of multiple media in the classroom, but it brings in its wake such fundamental changes in the learning process that a whole new approach to teacher training is called for.

Physical factors to be considered in computer use

Little attention has been focused so far on physical factors concerned with the regular use of IT in primary education. It is time that parents, teachers and educational authorities took a closer interest in the long-term physical effects that working on an adult-size computer may have on the health and well-being of our children - my short visit around Europe left me with some uncomfortable images in regards to the position of computers and the posture of children. Specifications could be drawn up by hardware producers on the recommended height of the computer screen and the keyboard, in reference to the average height of users at a given age. The size of the keyboard and mouse could also be better adapted for young users. It is surprising that no concerted efforts have been made in this direction so far. The shared use of headphones is another health factor that deserves closer attention, and little has been said to date about the type of filters that should be attached to the screen if we are to protect our children from toxic rays, yet the alert has already been given on extensive use of computers by pregnant women. A far greater effort should be made in terms of comfort, health and posture if children are to have frequent access to computers at an early age - according to present estimations, many of them will spend several hours per week for at least five decades working on a computer!

IT pollution

The NCET has published an interesting brochure for parents advising on choice of material and the dangers of allowing a child to remain in front of his computer for long periods to the detriment of social interactions with his environment. Parents are also alerted to the dangers of unsupervised access to Internet (and the growing incidence of propaganda from extremist groups, lessons on how to make a bomb, discussion groups on "anti-conformist" values that could perturb young people and eventually jeopardise democracy). The new information highway server, America On Line, has introduced a means of

---

39. Marbeau V., Les perpectives offertes par l'informatique et les technologies de la communication, in *La Revue de l'EPI*, N°79, Paris, EPI, 1995, p. 104.
40. Hart B., Holt G., Fletcher C., Tyldesley A., *Extending Horizons*, U.K., NCET, 1994

overcoming this problem with a one-for-four subscription scheme. The subscription holder has full access to Internet, but limits access rights for the other three users by means of a code. Is regulation at last dawning in the Information Age?

IT educational software that is not really relevant to the task in hand can also produce negative effects on learning. Before introducing IT into a subject area, teachers are urged to ask themselves "What does IT make possible that would have been impossible before?[40]" Poorly-adapted applications can waste time and leave children confused as to what is really being asked of them.

Few behavioural problems have been linked to the use of the computer, despite the fact that children work in groups around a computer often located in an unsupervised classroom. Talking is said to be "busy" talking and children set enthusiastically about their tasks, concentrating on one task for much longer periods than usual. As with all things, the secret of effective use lies with the user. If teachers are given the opportunity to discover adapted organisational methods and develop new pedagogical skills that naturally incorporate IT into their teaching practice, if they are encouraged to develop greater insights into the value of interactions brought about by the use of IT and recognize it's the potential to free them from certain routine tasks and enable them to individualise their teaching methods to cater to the differences in skills and aptitudes in their learners, then certainly the advantages will outweigh any negative effects that the use of IT may have.

SECTION THREE

Confronting the Information Age

"You can tell a good craftsman by the quality of his tools."

ANONYMOUS

Chapter 8

Implementing IT
in European primary education

Government-implemented programs

The issues and problems regarding change in the educational system are complex and multi-faceted, and the integration of IT in primary schools is no exception. Its successful implementation directly depends upon implementation strategies, which should take into account not just the amount of equipment to be made available, but also long-term projections and goals consistent with an overview of the intended role and use of the technology across the school. People at all levels need more help in formulating clear policies if they are to take full advantage of the potential impact of IT on pupils' learning[1]. Many pitfalls have been encountered in the past, due to poor choice of material that becomes rapidly superseded, material that remains locked in a cupboard because teachers are unwilling or incapable of using it, poorly located or distributed material, unsuitable software, discouragement from headmasters and school board members who don't understand the full implications of IT on pupils' learning, sporadic projects that start up then die out due to lack of funds and/or insufficient means of assessment.

Implementation methods vary from country to country. Some countries supply computers and software in large quantities for specific projects (e.g. Integrated Learning Systems, CD-ROM's in the UK) then follow up with in-depth project assessment before extending the application nation-wide. Others leave the decision and financing to local bodies, then provide a national pedagogical advisory service to support its use (e.g. SCRIPT in Luxembourg).

The MINERVA project in Portugal

Portugal set up a nation-wide project in 1985 to implement Information Technology as a catalyst to induce far-reaching and long-needed changes at all levels of education. MINERVA (Means of Informatics in Education: Rationalisation, Valorisation, Actualisation) was run by an interactive and collaborative triangle comprising the Portuguese Ministry of Education, 25 local

---

1. Cox M.J., Johnson D.C., *The ImpacT Report*, London, King's College, 1993, p.166

organisations called "Nodes" (staffed by university professors and seconded teachers) and approximately 1,000 schools (50 to 90 schools per Node). It aimed at harnessing the commitment of teachers and university professors to generate a spirit of research into both curriculum and pedagogy. Intermediary structures called CALs (Local Support Centres) were created to serve as resource centres and provide neighbouring schools with equipment, training and support. Training was mainly carried out on the cascade model by seconded teachers working in Nodes. Although the project was born in an initial wave of IT enthusiasm, it was finally disbanded in 1994 due to lack of funding, inadequate assessment methods and marginalisation by the government[2]. OECD-appointed independent experts called in by Portuguese authorities in 1994 to assess the results of the MINERVA project, state that it has produced six distinct gains in the national education system. It has succeeded in:

- fostering engagement, exploration and energy
- bridging the gap between city and country, past and present
- creating a better understanding of the natural world
- teaching staff to work in teams
- better serving children with special needs
- catalysing a broader pattern of change.

It has also left 4% of Portuguese primary schools with an average child/computer ratio of 50:1, an efficient network of CALs and a lot of discouraged but determined teachers sufficiently trained to be able to continue with their own IT projects in class.

A highly centralised implementation system

PRINT (Project Group for the Introduction of New Technology) is the implementation team set up in the Netherlands within the framework of the Comenius* operation. Comenius, run jointly by the Ministry of Education, the Society of Dutch Municipalities and the five national organisations governing the different educational bodies (Catholic schools, Protestant schools, etc.), is a national project initiated in the aim of improving the quality and effectiveness of the Dutch educational system. Between 1990 and 1994, it installed in schools a total of 27,000 computers and 9,000 printers free of charge. Deliveries are co-ordinated by a Steering Committee, a Project Office deals with day-to-day business and schools can telephone a Project Bureau for information during working hours.

In order to avoid problems of simultaneous double innovation in education, the initial phase of the PRINT project is primarily intended to introduce the computer as a new technological medium into primary and special schools; a

---

2. OECD, DEPGEF, *Report of the MINERVA Project Evaluators*, Lisbon, Ministry of Education, 1994
* A national project in the Netherlands, not to be confused with the EEC's "Comenius" in the SOCRATES program

second phase will focus on using that medium to improve the quality of education. PRINT works through advisory centres (responsible for support to participating schools and the realisation of professional knowledge-enlarging measures) and teacher training colleges (courses to help activity co-ordinators and in conjunction with courseware supply). Specific aims are to enlarge expertise of school teams through training courses that will:

- provide an introduction to/orientation toward computer use in class
- develop awareness of realistic and practical applications in CAI/CMI
- give insight into the consequences connected to the introduction of IT
- train teachers in the best use of IT for themselves and their pupils
- train teachers in the use of subject specific applications

PRINT is also responsible for the introduction of software (both educational and administrative software to facilitate the organisational tasks of the teaching team), the development of new courseware, the creation of a host system to network regional support centres and the setting up of a suitable advisory and information system.

The project is highly centralised in that all participating schools (today a total of 9,800, representing 99% of all Dutch schools) must complete a three-year work cycle, and all begin the implementation stage with a standard hardware and software starter package that includes a program called SIS -

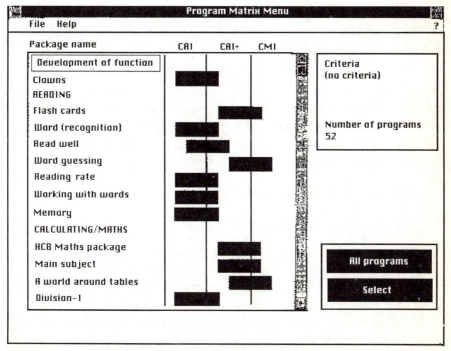

A SCREEN FROM THE PROGRAM MATRIX

"software in relation" (described below and already mentioned in relation to DOCO, Chapter 5) and a program matrix. The program matrix (see figure below) lists all available software, giving a CAI, CAI+ or CMI rating on all exercise types per program and an indication of curriculum relevance and age level suitability. The matrix is updated twice a year; the most recent version contains data on more than 200 programs.

In the aim of upgrading assessment methods in order to allow class and head teachers to monitor pupil progress more closely, particularly in light of the Netherlands' general educational policy to reduce the number of pupils sent to special schools from 4% to 2%, the SIS serves as a means of connection between packages (for class lists, pupil library skills through the DOCO software, etc.), helps teachers in task-based selection of software and permits coded-level access which increases in keeping with user expertise. It includes a pupil-progress mapping facility that links individual pupil improvement to what pupils at a set age can normally do. When a child moves to a new school his computerised records follow, and the class teacher makes every effort to continue the work program begun in the previous school. The system provides for the computerisation of the overall tasks and operations of schools, giving an overview of what tasks are carried out, who does them and how long each task takes. The aim is to streamline administrative duties to leave more time for individualised teaching, to free the teacher in order that he may better serve his class and "keep his finger on the pulse" of each of his pupils. An added advantage of introducing a centralised system is that it has coerced almost all national publishers into accepting a standard data form for the programs they publish.

In the Netherlands, the choice to introduce computers in a school is a joint decision that must be taken by mutual agreement between class teachers, head teachers, administrative staff and members of the school board. Every one of these persons has his own active role to play in the three-year training cycle, completion of which is a compulsory condition for any school wishing to participate in the Comenius operation (Chapter 9).

A decentralised implementation system

In France a decentralisation law was passed in 1983 giving entire responsibility to local municipalities for the installation and upkeep of teaching equipment in schools. However, in 1985, the state launched the project "Informatique pour tous" ("computers for all" though the project involved, in fact, the installation of 2,000 computer laboratories for schools throughout the whole of France), intended to provide computer, printer and software access to all school children over the age of 9. The computer laboratories, generally consisting of six workstations linked to a central server, were usually shared by several schools. Teachers therefore had to take their class to the computer laboratory, sometimes at quite a distance from the school, if they were to give their pupils the required IT access. In preparation for the installation of this equipment, 100,000 teachers took part in a one-week intensive training course over a period of 4 months. The project placed an emphasis on computer use in the science/technology curriculum, to a large extent concentrating on CAI and LOGO. It was formally requested that every child have a minimum access of 50 hours before leaving elementary school. A protocol introduced two years later made the equipment the property of municipalities, who once again become responsible for all maintenance, replacement, new purchases, etc. of equipment.

Since then the implementation system has become completely decentralised, the extent to which IT is used in schools often depends largely on the interest shown by municipalities and the driving force of the Academy Inspector in charge of that area. Although two government services exist to aid in the implementation of IT in schools, a bottom-up system has developed in which individual teachers or small groups create their own software, applications and pedagogical approaches, knowing full well that they will confront major difficulties if they are hoping to gain recognition for their efforts or wish to reproduce their pilot projects on a wider scale.

In 1991, a new teacher training effort went into operation - 450 primary school teachers were relieved of their teaching functions to follow an IT training course which would enable them to train other teachers on a cascade model. Today almost 1,100 of these "computer advisors" are working full- or part-time in the primary sector. Since 1992, with the advent of cheaper, more user-friendly hardware and general-purpose software and a shift in emphasis in the primary curriculum - competence in native language skills is now the priority - word processing and communication through modem have become one of the prime fields of activity.

A cross-border collaboration in Nordic countries

Sweden, Norway, Finland and Denmark collaborate closely to give their respective education systems the best possible conditions for implementation of Information Technology. Twice a year, four to six software programs from each country are pooled, translated then presented in catalogue form by the Nordic council, set up in the aim of disseminating educational software. A common platform is used by all software publishers to simplify the task of translation into the four languages.

In Finland, a new educational strategy was recently drafted by the Minister of Education setting the goal to network all schools in the country by the year 2000. A second goal is for all future teachers to undergo a 5-week IT training course as part of their initial training program. Already approximately 1,000 teachers per year take part in IT-oriented in-service training courses, though it is considered that the most efficient training model is the unofficial transfer of knowledge that takes place between colleagues.

The major part of the Ministry's budget is spent on research. No nation-wide implementation program has been set up since the strategy is for schools to draw up their own plans. When these are accepted by the Department of Education, 50% of the total cost of equipment is reimbursed.

The role of associations and volunteer workers

One of the most striking features in all of the projects observed during this study is the key role played by non-profit making organisations, parents and retired professionals. A great number of teachers, too, consecrate evenings, weekends and holidays to develop their own projects, raise funds for equipment and even attend conferences and take training courses abroad at their own expense in order to successfully integrate IT in their classrooms. Throughout Europe, IT implementation has become almost a "cottage industry". Those with sufficient interest and civic conscience to realise the major issue that is at stake in our democracy are striving to make up for the inaction displayed by education policy makers. We shall now take a look at the work carried out by three associations: one in France and another in Luxembourg have been set up by teachers, the third, in Belgium, is the brainchild of a retired professional.

The E.P.I. in France

The E.P.I (Public Schooling and Informatics), an association created by a group of teachers in 1971, publishes a quarterly revue that represents a vital communication link for teachers seeking information on IT innovations, pedagogical approach, training courses or wishing to exchange software through the "software stock market" that the E.P.I. team introduced some years ago. Today the association is striving to reach the 80% of schools in France that are still not using IT, due to:

- reticence on the part of teachers
- lack of training (IT is still not included in initial teacher training cursus, except for a short word processing course at the end of the final year; although practising teachers have the right to 3 days of training per year, very few computer-oriented courses are available)
- lack of equipment
- lack of software (given the limited French-speaking market in Europe, publishers are not keen to invest)

The vocation of the association is to offer every child equal learning opportunities in a country in which it is estimated that 1 million people are handicapped by illiteracy, a problem that will only be accentuated by the information age. E.P.I. has set itself a number of highly pertinent goals:

> - continue to encounter those in charge of education to convince them to act, on the grounds that education is a public service with a responsibility to answer to the expectations of pupils and the needs of society
> - set an example by offering teachers intermediary solutions which will encourage them to embark on the IT adventure
> - for those already convinced, act as a watchdog over ultra-rapid evolutions (all new technology is presented as a miraculous remedy to the ills of society, but no technology is without its disadvantages)
> - serve as a constant reminder that educational software is a cultural product intricately linked with language, methods and values, and that the time and money needed to produce multimedia products could lead to economic and ideological domination. On the other hand, software development could represent a sound government investment since production costs would eventually be counteracted by a reduction in teaching costs and added value for all school subjects and activities[3].

The A.P.T.I.C.E. in Luxembourg

The A.P.T.I.C.E. (Association for the Promotion of Information Technology and Communication in Schools) in Luxembourg, works closely with other national education services in its quest to develop national awareness of the importance of IT in education. It was recently called upon by the National Minister of Education to put forward proposals on the introduction of a national policy, taking into account the key role that IT will play in the future of education. The association aims at providing IT access for every child at all levels of education and to awaken teachers to the enormous potential that IT offers as a means of promoting an education based on an active exchange of ideas and interests in both Luxemburgish and foreign languages. It places particular emphasis on the value of IT as a means of developing independent learning skills through the differentiation of structures and methods used in class, at the same time clearly underlining the necessity to promote group work and group solidarity by developing the competencies of each individual and encouraging the transfer of skills between pupils. A.P.T.I.C.E. suggests that a pluridisciplinary approach be adopted that will actively involve pupils and focus on their authentic centres of interest in the aim of replying to the needs of a society in evolution and taking into account the social, cultural and economic interdependence that exists in today's society. In light of this last objective, it is not surprising to learn that the class teacher responsible for the "open-ended learning approach" observation described earlier is an active member of this association.

---

3. Dossiers de presse, in *La revue de l'association E.P.I.*, Paris, September 1995, p. 35 - 40

A.P.T.I.C.E. also considers that IT training in initial and in-service teacher courses is essential if schools are to confront the challenges of the modern world and maintain their institutional role in society. Several members conduct optional teacher training modules that can be taken as part of the cursus for the Teacher's higher certificate. At present, the association is running workshops in a number of primary schools as a means of giving as many teachers as possible a realistic insight into how IT can be integrated into their current teaching practice. One long-term objective is to set up telecomputer networks that could serve both as a means of promoting access to training courses and as a communication mode to encourage professional dialogue - the common cry from teachers in all corners of Europe is the need to pool and exchange ideas with counterparts through telecomputer networks.

A project conducted by retired professionals

Although this project in a secondary school in Basse-Wavre (Belgium) concerns 13 year-old children, I have included it in this report for three reasons. Firstly, it offers a perfect example of the way in which volunteer workers can use the expertise and experience gained through their professional career to open up new horizons for schools. Secondly, the multi-media material produced in this class will subsequently be used by other children and teachers as a reference resource. And finally, because educationalists in Switzerland have expressed interest in using it as a model to set up similar projects in Geneva.

The project is the inspiration of Mr Francis Legae who, having been forced into early retirement through structural changes in the company he was working for, was seeking a way in which he could put the experience he had gained in the information sector to the service of the community and, more particularly, to help today's generation confront the challenges presented by new technology. In collaboration with Mrs Eliane Jacques, also a volunteer worker, he set up his own association, named CREADIM, and drafted a project which would introduce school children to the use of IT, and develop their awareness of the importance of sound, image and interactivity to communicate ideas. Obviously, the major handicap was lack of equipment. One day Mr Legae was walking through an exhibition hall in a trade fair when he got into a conversation with a representative of a major hardware producer. One idea led to another, and several weeks later the company promised to lend the material necessary to set up a computer laboratory in a school of his choice. That was three years ago. Today, the association is running projects in three Belgian schools in the subject areas of history, geography, science, religion, music, technology and French.

In the class in which our observation was carried out, the project has been incorporated as a 12-hour module (6 sessions of 2 hours) into the science

On-site Observation
GRID N° 10

SCHOOL/CLASS:	Basse-Wavre - Belgium - Year 2 (13 yr-olds)
DATE:	26/11/1995
RELEVANCE OF IT:	Multimedia is used to build group projects on science topic (Energy) in relation to last year's topic - Environment
PROGRAM USED:	Picture Book by Digithurst (U.K.)
COMPUTER DISTRIBUTION:	Network of 8 IBM PS1, 1 computer linked to TV monitor for teacher, scanner for images
INTERACTION ALLOWED BY SOFTWARE:	Due to limited time (12 hours) teacher inputs screen set-ups, chn add in captions & pictures. Screen feedback when problems occur. Group interaction is high around computer, before & after computer sessions
VARIETY OF ACTIVITIES TAKING PLACE SIMULTANEOUSLY:	Organisation skills are important to create basic network schema for popups, chn refer repeatedly to schema; negotiating, reading & selecting material brought from home, formulating & typing texts
TEACHER PURPOSE (3 CULTURES):	Science & technology
GROUP WORK/TEAM SPIRIT:	High collaborative spirit. Chn start information search at home, choose their partners ("he's creative but I write better texts"), work enthusiastically to help group. Peer-correction to produce perfect results
SENSE OF RESPONSIBILITY/ PERSONAL DISCIPLINE:	Each of the 7 groups are working on a complementary module for a final class project to be kept for use in school, each is aware of his responsibility in overall effort. Whole class is very busy throughout lesson
DEGREE OF DECISION-MAKING/COMMITMENT/WILL INGNESS TO TAKE RISKS:	With more time chn could be responsible for their own page set-up to increase decision-making opportunities. They are highly committed, but somewhat hindered by time and pre-designed page
SENSE OF INITIATIVE/ CURIOSITY/CREATIVITY:	One group turned science into poetry, scanning images to make a frieze. Limitation for curiosity due to time restriction, though one child went to Greenpeace for information. Addition of sound would be an advantage
DEGREE OF ATOMISATION/ SOCIALISATION:	High socialisation within groups through input of ideas, correction, working with teacher in more collaborative way
SENSE OF ACHIEVEMENT/ PRIDE IN WORK:	Very pleased with professional standard results which are handed on to future classes as teaching resource
CORRESPONDENCE TO PURPOSE/LEVEL OF ACHIEVEMENT IN CULTURE:	Good use of technology, limited by short length of project; requires efficient use of reference material and provides practice in expressing ideas in a limited space

Background grid page 146.

program. The object is to create multi-media software on sources of energy, a theme which is related to studies carried out the previous year on the environment. The seven groups of two to four children have each chosen a different but complementary energy source to investigate, with energy types ranging from solar, wind and hydro-electric to natural gas and nuclear energy. The software used, *Picture Book*, enables pupils to present their work in a network-type organisation with a main page leading to more detailed descriptions on production and use of energy, each page providing a number of "pop-ups" of images and texts. Unfortunately no resource material is kept in the computer laboratory so children have had to bring in their own reference material, usually from home but also from the public and school libraries.

The laboratory is equipped with a network of eight IBM PS1 computers, one of which is linked to a TV monitor for the teacher to use when she wishes to demonstrate a point to the whole class. A fund-raising campaign was run by voluntary workers last year for the purchase of a much-needed scanner, which now serves to streamline the process of incorporating images. As only one computer is equipped with recording facilities, projects in this class do not yet incorporate sound.

The learning gains from this IT experience are multiple. First and foremost, the organisation of screens into a tree-like structure draws on a number of information handling skills that, in most cases, are quite new to children of this age. It leads them to reflect upon and examine more closely the organisation and connectedness of information in general, and that of information technology resources in particular. How can we expect a multi-media publishing industry to develop under favourable conditions if children are not introduced to the new skills needed at an early age? It is unfortunate that, because of the 12-hour time limit, the pupils cannot exploit organisational opportunities to the fullest; at the moment they set up their page distribution and layout on paper so that the teacher and Mr Legae can enter the blank schema into the computer between lessons.

A second learning gain is in language precision. Because of the limited space available for written and visual explanations, the pupils discover the need for pertinence and precision in what they write. By this age they have already been taught the art of précis writing, now they have a concrete example of why it is necessary to summarise in certain situations. Interactivity was particularly strong in the groups observed; every word and image must be negotiated if the finished project is to meet the approval of all group members and include all essential data in just 10 or so pages. Motivation is high as learning has a specific purpose, every participant is aware that there is an audience awaiting his production and that if his module is to be part of a program that will serve as a reference resource on energy in future years it must be clear, interesting, well-written and factually correct. Pupils are hence encouraged to take greater care on an aesthetic level. One group, three girls working on wind as a source of energy, wrote their captions in the form of poetry and used a scanned image to create a frieze across the top of the page, adapting *Picture Book* to meet their needs in much the same way as the class in France used *Smalltalk* to create wallpaper. IT in this case has provided the means to turn science into poetry and the school into an area of enriching learning experiences rather than a machine to execute the rigid procedures[4] so often connected with teaching the hard facts of science.

The activities of these two voluntary workers, however, go much further than supplying equipment, helping teachers in class and setting up computer screens to streamline the tasks of teachers and learners. CREADIM trains teachers who wish to work on this type of project, helps them choose modules that can be developed in class, and promotes the use of multi-media as a means of creating learning resources both in Belgium and abroad. If we take into account the remarks of the teacher in the class visited at Basse-Wavre, we can see that their efforts are highly appreciated: "I could never have introduced this module if it had not been for Mr Legae, I didn't even know very much about using computers and could never have used one in class without his backing and support. The project takes up a lot of free time but it is worth it when we see the motivation of even (or most particularly) the poorer students. When children handle their own text, image and sound, they develop a new understanding of the strategies of the media... the module is far too short and should become a subject in its own right rather than being squeezed into science."

*

* *

Associations have always been an enriching element in the social fabric of western societies. In education, they represent a vital means of actively involving people from all walks of life in the educational process and in bringing real-life experiences gained in widely diverse professional sectors to the service of the community. Parent-teacher associations are playing a major role, too, not only in organising fund raising events to equip schools with hardware and software, but also by putting pressure on educational authorities to integrate into their schools the methods that they have seen used in other areas and other countries. A number of the pilot sites visited during this study testify to the unsparing efforts that non-teacher members of the community are investing for the integration of IT in education.

---

4. Papert S., *The Children's Machine: Rethinking School in the Age of the Computer*, New York, Harvester/Wheatsheaf, 1993, p.70

Chapter 9

Integrating IT
into current teaching practice

*"Teaching is probably the only profession in the twentieth century that would permit
a person from the nineteenth century to walk into today's world and recommence
practising without any adaptation period or further training"*

R. BIBEAU *National Ministry of Education, Quebec*[5]

The qualities of an IT-competent teacher

What is the profile of the teacher able to effectively integrate the information tools of our era into his current teaching practice? If we compare the qualities of the teachers encountered during this study, we realise that they have several points in common:

- an awareness of the need to *acknowledge and cater to the differences in learning rhythm and aptitude of their pupils*. In all cases, this can be attributed to one (or more) of four factors ; 1) positive (though sometimes negative) learning experiences during their own educational cursus; 2) ideas sparked through reading pedagogical literature or as a result of initial or in-service training courses and developed through personal effort and the firm conviction that the school should do more in providing equal learning opportunities for all; 3) contact with innovative colleagues on the same teaching team, through membership of an association or club, or through electronic network links; 4) "persuasion" and support from teacher trainers, head teachers, inspectors and colleagues.

- the ability to *apply a research reasoning method*, "learning by doing", to find the right tools and adapt their teaching style to suit the needs of their pupils and the reality of today's world. This method cannot be learnt in a 3 or 4-year initial training course; it is gradually developed through the teacher's own learning experiences at an early age, or sometimes force-fed through "master-apprentice" contact with scientific researchers at the level of higher university studies.

5. Bibeau R., Attention! Passage étroit - «Autoroute pédagogique», in *La revue de l'association EPI*, Paris, September 1995, p. 163

Education is a vicious circle. Unless the teacher is stimulated by a strong external influence, he will reproduce the methods and role models he himself has encountered during his own learning experiences. Applying a research method in class implies that the teacher has the self-confidence to learn by his own errors as well as by his successes, alongside his pupils, with his pupils, and even from his pupils. By admitting to his pupils that he is not an infallible fountain of knowledge, he frees his pupils from the fear of errors and encourages them to embark on their own quest for knowledge.

• *a pragmatic view of teaching and sufficient organisational flexibility* to create a learner-directed environment in which children set about their own learning tasks enthusiastically and independently. A teacher is no longer someone who just "gives lessons"; he is rather someone who organises, observes, stimulates, assesses and fosters the various learning processes in children, ready to take remedial action whenever necessary[6]. On the sites observed, the computer served as a medium between the pupils and teacher, stimulating the learning process for the children whilst freeing the teacher to provide individualised attention when necessary and enabling him to "keep his finger on the pulse" of all children at once. Work at the computer is necessarily carried out in pairs or small groups, and often several activities are taking place in the class at once - this offers an enormous challenge in terms of organisational capacity for teachers.

• an *aptitude for communication, social relations and teamwork*, evident in pupil/teacher contact in class, which goes far beyond the traditional teacher-directed dialogue prevalent in so many classes. The outstanding feature in most of the classrooms I visited is that there is no outward sign of teacher "authority" - children and teacher work and learn together, conversing as equals as they set about finding the best means to go about a task, assess results, set new learning goals. The atmosphere in the classroom is relaxed but busy, the pupil/teacher relationship is reflected in the way children quietly discuss problems and help each other. Parent volunteers are included as part of the class. Other teachers "drop in" to discuss their difficulties - usually IT-related. It should be added that most of the teachers encountered during the study seem to have assumed a natural role of IT co-ordinator in their school, simply because the rest of the staff know they have a successful project underway.

A teacher who remains closed in the microcosm of his classroom has no incentive to implement change; it is only through a positive educational climate between teaching staff that he can continue his own lifelong learning experience. If he cannot appreciate the advantages of teamwork himself, he will have little incentive to encourage teamwork in his pupils. IT-competent teachers

---

6. Council for Cultural Co-operation: School Education Division, *Innovation in Primary Education*, Strasbourg, Council of Europe, 1988, p.40

list professional dialogue as being one of the major factors that enabled them to evolve towards a new style of teaching. All decry the lack of opportunities provided to exchange ideas on new teaching approaches with colleagues in other parts of their own country and in Europe.

> • a *supportive hierarchy* ready to encourage innovative efforts and adapt curriculum requirements to leave the teacher more freedom to choose the tools and methods he uses in class.

These qualities correspond closely to several points underlined in the findings of the CERI (Centre for Educational Research and Innovation), an organisation created by the OECD council in 1968 and commissioned to carry out a study on the use of IT in education in the late eighties. The CERI suggests that a teacher wishing to use IT widely in class should:

> - know how to run and maintain the systems used,
> - learn to understand the uses of IT through discussions with scientists and educational specialists,
> - gain insight into appropriate pedagogical applications of IT. In particular, to develop a sense of how to use the technology in the aim of helping pupils acquire learning strategies, a strong perception of his own value and a spirit of co-operation,
> - be receptive to the messages communicated during the use of IT,
> - keep up with recent evolutions in science and technology,
> - be ready to spend the time necessary to reflect upon traditional teaching methods, teaching philosophy and the organisation of the learning environment[7].

It seems, then, that it is not simply short in-service courses on the use of IT that will permit teachers to successfully integrate IT in their teaching practice. Nor is it an IT module added to an already overloaded initial training course. Teachers must be given the opportunity to develop new teaching styles by discovering for themselves the utility of IT in their own learning experiences and, for trainee teachers, through encounters with staff at teachers' college and during practice sessions who will provide valid models and from whom they may learn the "new" role of teachers. Governments, teacher-training institutions, local authorities, head teachers, school board members and parents - all are involved in the integration process. Radical changes must be made at all levels!

Initial teacher training

Teaching is an Art. Indeed, it is surprising that we apply the term "training" as if we were talking about learning skills that can be applied automatically, and

---

7. CERI, *Information Technologies and Basic Learning*, Paris, OECD, 1987, p. 197

not "education" which would imply the development of knowledge and reasoning. The role of the teacher is to develop in his pupils the capacity to become independent lifelong learners. If we go one step further, teachers should already be independent lifelong learners, if not teachers' training college perhaps represents the last opportunity to develop this capacity. The contents of initial training courses should be modified with these goals in mind:

- give a greater insight into the pedagogical approaches that can be used to individualise teaching to cater to the specific needs of pupils, and the importance of IT in this process.
- create a pupil-directed (not a teacher-directed) learning environment
- provide opportunities for pupils to learn through an active research method, developing at the same time their capacity for reasoning
- develop greater proficiency in organisational methods that will allow new teachers to integrate IT into class work, and encourage pupil interactions that will enhance the learning environment
- develop the art of cross-curricular learning, allowing children to make their own associations that will render new skills and learning more meaningful
- enable teachers to apply new assessment methods that will help pupils to set their own learning objectives.
- develop an aptitude for communication and teamwork
- continue in their own learning process through effective use of professional literature, on-line data sources and meaningful exchanges with colleagues.

Competence alone, however, is not enough. Teachers also need adequate support and encouragement from head teachers, parents and colleagues if they are to use IT effectively in class. They also need to be given the time necessary to learn to use new technologies, sufficient access to resources and the possibility to communicate easily with colleagues who are working on similar projects[8].

A need for in-service training

Initial teacher training courses incorporate a number of practice periods during which trainee teachers go into the classrooms of experienced teachers to learn their métier in what can be described as a master/apprentice system similar to that used to train craftsmen in the days of old. This is a valuable system that could also be used to advantage in the pupil/teacher relationship[9], on condition that the master is an "expert" in the skills to be acquired. Yet, in a recent survey

---

8. CERI, *Information Technologies and Basic Learning*, Paris, OECD, 1987, p. 197
9. Delacôte G., *Savoir apprendre: les nouvelles méthodes*, Paris, Editions Odile Jacob, 1996, p.155-158

carried out on 800 teachers in France[10] (58% were aged over 40), **2/3 of the sample population consider that their prime objective is to teach pupils the 3 R's** and only 1/4 expressed a wider conception of the transfer of knowledge as "focusing on stimulating the desire to learn". When asked if they would use IT more often if the material was available, 47% said yes to audio-visual material, 31% yes to computers. The survey adds that this attitude to computers is seemingly because few teachers feel capable of sufficiently mastering computer skills. How can we continue to train teachers in this way if the knowledge of the "experts", their objectives and their methods, no longer answer the needs of our modern society?

This survey, representative of the situation in most European countries according to the results of the Ampère study, highlights two important factors: firstly, a minority of teachers are aware of a wider conception of learning and, secondly, few feel capable of, or even wish to, use IT in their teaching practice. Hence there is an urgent need to train the 4 million teachers currently teaching in Europe. The contents of in-service courses should focus on the same methods and objectives as those listed for initial training courses.

Widely diverse training projects are currently underway in Europe. We shall now examine more closely two of these.

A year-long preparation cycle for the entire staff

Innovation in primary school is a process that involves all levels in the educational hierarchy; the Comenius project takes this aspect into account in its training cycle. The decision to join Comenius is not one that is taken lightly in the Netherlands. It requires a concerted training effort for all members of the staff for a full year even before the implementation process begins. Before starting the cycle, the staff is required to make an analysis of the tasks that the computer will be used for once it has been delivered (the following year). The head teacher and a member of the school board then attend a half-day information meeting, organised by the regional advisory centre each year in May or June, where they will learn more about the PRINT procedure, the implications of the soft- and hardware standard, what will be supplied by the project and how the conditions for delivery and use can be achieved, an explanation of the work cycle and answers to questions specific to their school.

Early in the next school year, head teachers are invited to attend a short course (approximately 16 hours) where they will be assisted in drawing up a school policy, advised on the implications of introducing a new medium such as IT in their schools, and helped to assess their own role and that of the activity co-ordinator. They also receive information on training and support programs

---

10. Survey carried out by CREDOC in France, June 1994

for their teaching team. Head teachers can continue their training by attending subject-specific workshops.

One staff member is chosen as activity co-ordinator, responsible for co-ordinating activities in the school, supporting practical aspects of computer use, assisting the staff in specific educational and didactic aspects in computer use, and helping them to choose workshops adapted to their needs. This person attends eight half-day training meetings, from October to February, where he will receive instruction material to be made available in his school and develop the expertise necessary to carry out his duties.

The fourth step in the preparation cycle consists of eight half-hour television broadcasts destined to provide the teaching staff with a clear view of the practical possibilities for computer use in schools. Individual team members may also attend regional workshops on specific computer and software uses. In April, staff members attend an information market where they can acquaint themselves with hard- and software applications in order to make an informed choice. The team then specifies the activities to be organised in an implementation plan. The last step in the preparation cycle is a study day where head teachers and activity co-ordinators learn to use the program matrix, discussed in chapter 8. Of course, once the equipment has been installed the work cycle has not ended. For the next two years, an ongoing training effort is required of teachers as they learn to use this new teaching medium. The activity co-ordinator keeps staff informed on software-specific workshops run by PRINT, and the Project Office and Project Bureau are just a phone call away to cope with integration problems. As teachers gradually learn to master the SIS software, they are given access to new levels to help them in their administrative tasks. The regularly updated program matrix keeps them informed on new software - beyond the starter package all new acquisitions are up to the school.

The Comenius work cycle is an interesting training model that combines co-operation and co-ordination. It develops a team spirit within the school since each staff member is a vital link in the final decision-making process.

Distance training

The Northamptonshire Distance In-Service Training project - INSET Cluster - in the UK began as a teacher training project and soon turned into an invaluable communication link between teachers in 8 geographically-isolated one or two-teacher schools, parent/teacher associations and children. Originally the multimedia computers were installed complete with an electronic network link and a CD-ROM of text-based teacher training material to examine how this model might prove to be more cost-effective than other training models, change

On-site Observation
GRID N° 11

SCHOOL/CLASS:	Grendon Primary School, Northamptonshire - UK
DATE:	06/06/1995
RELEVANCE OF IT:	Use of IT to develop interaction between 8 geographically-isolated schools in region
PROGRAM USED:	Electronic interface used for e-mail & conferencing facilities, CD-ROM of existing text-based material (from NIAS) for teacher training purposes
COMPUTER DISTRIBUTION:	One multimedia computer per school, located near existing telephone socket (e.g. in staff room/head teacher's office)
INTERACTION ALLOWED BY SOFTWARE:	On a one-to-one basis between teachers, teacher/training, advisory & resource centres, parent/teacher delegates, pupil/pupil
VARIETY OF ACTIVITIES TAKING PLACE SIMULTANEOUSLY:	Not applicable
TEACHER PURPOSE (3 CULTURES):	Originally intended for science training, now provides an important information handling system covering all domains
GROUP WORK/TEAM SPIRIT:	Greater co-operation between teachers in 1 or 2-teacher schools & geographically-isolated colleagues, but also with parent associations and between pupils who maintain contact with friends met at cluster functions
SENSE OF RESPONSIBILITY/ PERSONAL DISCIPLINE:	All parties concerned consider that a new relationship has developed in which each party (teachers, parent associations, training & resource centres, children) makes every effort to further work of colleagues
DEGREE OF DECISION-MAKING/COMMITMENT/WILL INGNESS TO TAKE RISKS:	Improved decision-making through easier communication, a new opening to outside world. New ideas are discussed, collaboration opens new horizons
SENSE OF INITIATIVE/ CURIOSITY/CREATIVITY:	Better, more creative use of shared resources and ideas. Schools can afford more expensive projects as costs are shared (e.g. hire of a space laboratory to be visited by all schools in cluster)
DEGREE OF ATOMISATION/ SOCIALISATION:	Socialisation greatly developed in formerly isolated agricultural communities; teachers can work together, children can develop contacts made at cluster functions. Children are now using word-processing & modem to publish joint newsletter
SENSE OF ACHIEVEMENT/ PRIDE IN WORK:	Greater pride through improved communication & motivation & by the creation of community projects. All parties concerned (teachers/parents/ pupils) attempt to use new tools to the utmost to break down barriers caused by isolation
CORRESPONDENCE TO PURPOSE/LEVEL OF ACHIEVEMENT IN CULTURE:	Isolation has effectively been overcome, higher motivation in teachers will naturally lead to better learning conditions for children

Background grid page 141.

teachers' behaviour, improve pupil learning more effectively than traditional methods and be particularly relevant to the needs of small rural schools. The link provides interactive access to learning materials, expert advice (from NIAS - the Northamptonshire Inspection and Advisory Service), tutorial and peer support in the subject area of science, identified as the area of the new national curriculum where most training is needed.

Several of the teachers involved in the project had never used a computer before. Once the initial technical difficulties had been overcome, they began to explore the vast possibilities that this new communication tool could offer. Staff in the eight schools now work together to draw up their teaching program in science (in fact, this has been extended to all subjects), exchanging learning materials, pooling their funds to hire more expensive resource material that can be shared, (on the day of my visit the head teacher was negotiating the hire of a "space laboratory" that was to provide an occasion to unite several of the schools for a function day). Decision-making has improved through easier communication. The distance in-service training sessions continue and are considered to be most useful, but all teachers agree that the major gain for them has been the interactions that have resulted from using IT as a tool in their own learning experience and as an information handling system in all domains.

These interactions are described on four levels:

- teacher to teacher: the staff of the eight schools now feel less isolated and can draw on the experience of colleagues to cater more effectively to the demands of learners
- teacher to parent: parents in small rural areas often participate actively in the activities of the local schools. Now parents drop in to send an e-mail to co-ordinate meetings and activities with parents or teachers of other schools, and often stay on to help children send their own e-mail
- teacher to pupil: sensing that their teachers are highly motivated, pupils want to share this new learning experience
- pupil to pupil: children can now regularly communicate by e-mail with friends (met during joint projects run by the cluster of schools), exchange ideas and build projects together. Needless to say, because written expression has become a pleasure, a marked improvement has been noted in the work of many pupils.

Although the original objective of this distance learning project now appears to be of secondary importance, the project is considered by all participants as a major success. Through hands-on experience with IT for their own learning purposes, teachers have succeeded in enriching the learning environment for their pupils.

Regular on-site training with an IT co-ordinator

The role of IT co-ordinator varies from country to country. Sometimes the most technically competent teacher in the school is unofficially appointed by his colleagues to help out whenever there is a problem, to keep them informed on new software and applications, to disseminate information on training possibilities - he carries out the role of IT co-ordinator though often he receives neither remuneration nor time-off from his daily teaching duties for the services he renders. In other countries, this function is attributed to a member of the staff who has followed a special training course and is allotted a certain number of hours per week to assume extra responsibilities within the school.

Mr Casamenti's job description is somewhat different again. Originally a primary school teacher, six years ago he followed a training course organised by the Italian Ministry to promote the use of IT in education. Since then he has been seconded to the Ministry to carry out three major functions in the eight schools falling under his jurisdiction in the Bologna area of Italy:

- training teachers in technical and pedagogical aspects of computer use in primary education,
- working with teachers in class for an initial period until they develop sufficient autonomy to develop their own projects,
- running workshops for specific applications.

A computer laboratory has been set up in each of these eight schools, funded through government grants, local municipalities and fund-raising events organised by parents. Above and beyond his normal duties he develops software, worksheets and user manuals to meet the specific needs of his schools. He also calls on local organisations to help set up projects to extend the possibilities schools can offer. One such project is KIDSLINK, created with the support of the Bologna Municipality, a local radio astronomy institute and a computer club. The project aims at bringing students of Bologna schools in contact with students in other parts of the world to encourage communication with pupils from different cultural backgrounds and hence enhance the use of foreign languages via electronic links. In 1994 this experiment became nationwide and today counts more than one hundred schools as part of the network and KIDLINKS server. Through the mediation of an Italian teacher working in Manchester, several primary schools in England have now joined the network.

The INDIS project (Informatics and Discomforts) is another of his achievements. This project concerns all primary and secondary schools in the district and is aimed at:

- managing a software library and an informatics help desk,
- producing didactic units targeting children with difficulties

- updating and exchanging experiences and public property didactic software such as Leggo (reading), Scrivo (writing) and Puzzle (games for developing skills and logic).

The project is financed by the Emilia Romagna region and the four municipalities of the district.

This is yet another model of teacher training that could serve as an example for other countries.

*

*   *

If the teaching profession is considered to be a sector in crisis today[11], perhaps it is because insufficient effort has been made to provide the education system with the tools or the training necessary to keep up with the pace of progress. The economic sector has spared no means to equip every office with at least one computer, and most employees with long training courses to learn to use a word processor or a data base. When we consider the limited number of training courses on offer for teachers wishing to use IT as a learning tool, we realise that teachers have not been accorded equal opportunities - yet their role is vital for the future of all citizens and the future of our nations. A considerable budget has been accorded to large-scale training efforts in all other sectors of the economic world, why should the teaching profession be deprived of this means to update its methods and improve its performance?

11. Cochinaux, P., de Woot, P., *Moving Towards a Learning Society*, Geneva-Brussels, CRE-ERT, 1995, p.97

Chapter 10

Conclusion

The Information Age is today a reality - in most countries in Europe 10% of all households possess a computer. The school has been left behind in a movement that began more than a decade ago and is now gaining momentum. The professional sector depends heavily on Information Technology, children in the more privileged socio-professional categories use computers to do their homework, only the less favoured groups are being deprived of access to these new tools. IT today is somewhat like books in the 19th century, the citizens fortunate enough to possess them can extend their learning opportunities and thereby gain a natural advantage over the remainder of the population. But can Europe afford to pay the consequences of a two-speed society, with all the economic, social and civic factors that are at stake?

It is time for change. Why should a part of our population be deprived of an opportunity to secure their place in society?

As a result of this study, the Ampère Groupe recently submitted three recommendations to the European Union calling for:

1. the creation of a **European IT bureau** to accelerate integration in primary education
2. a concerted pan-European effort in the field of **teacher training**
3. the installation of sufficient **IT equipment** in every primary class in Europe

1) We strongly recommend that a European IT bureau be set up to carry out seven major functions:

• create **a data base** containing detailed information on the implementation methods used by Member States to integrate IT into the education system on a national level. Europe is rich in the diversity and complementarity of participating nations, this wealth should be put to the mutual advantage of all. Co-operation between nations already exists in this area and should be encouraged: Belgium has expressed a lively interest in the system used in the Netherlands; Nordic countries have, for several years, been pooling ideas and software in the economic interest and to the cultural advantage of the four nations concerned. This data base could serve as a source of reference to the countries still reluctant to introduce IT into schools.

• invite Member States to appoint an **IT co-ordinator** in every primary school establishment, relieved of a certain number of teaching hours and responsible for informing the European bureau of pilot projects in their school that could be worthy of further study and serve as a valuable source of ideas for participating nations. It has become evident throughout this study that the integration of IT is, in many countries, a bottom-up process, worthwhile projects often being brought to a halt through lack of material, funding or support from the educational hierarchy. An IT co-ordinator could centralise efforts and develop the notion of teamwork which has emerged as a driving factor in implementing new tools and new methods.

• create **a data base of pilot projects** underway or that could be set into operation if the necessary funds were made available. This could be made accessible to the IT co-ordinator in every school through an electronic network.

• **encourage worthwhile projects through financial support**. Competition is an essential vector in progress and could be put to use as a driving force in the integration of IT in schools. Portugal has set up a scheme whereby potential projects are submitted to a national agency in charge of IT implementation. A grant is allocated for the realisation of one project per year. A similar operation could be introduced on a European level.

• encourage participation of software publishers to set up **a data base of educational software**, accessible to IT co-ordinators for distribution to staff members in their school. The information contained in this data base should be drawn up in accordance with the norms stipulated by the European bureau and present reliable information on age level suitability, curriculum relevance, skills and methods applied. The program matrix developed by the Netherlands provides an excellent model of the way data on software can be recorded to facilitate the task of selection. One module of each software could be made available on-line as an added means of guiding teachers in their choice. This would develop the awareness of publishers as to the major responsibility they have in regards to the educational sector, and could provide the necessary incentive to unite their efforts to produce software in other European languages, consequently overcoming the problems of nations at an unfair disadvantage because of the limited number of people speaking their language.

• encourage Member States to set up **software lending libraries**, thereby providing teachers greater access to software such as that used in simulation and modelling. The price of task-oriented, subject-specific software which can often only be used for a short period each year in a class, puts it out of reach of many schools and thereby deprives children of educational opportunities that should be opened to them.

• provide up-to-date information on **training courses and seminars** that could promote European unity and professional (and cultural) exchanges in a sector in which professionals are only too often limited to the confines of their classroom. Training courses could be devised in such a way that participating teachers receive accreditation for the courses they successfully complete, in accordance with the suggestion put forward by the European Commission in the *Livre blanc sur l'éducation et la formation* on lifelong learning. In breaking down national barriers between teachers, and developing an awareness of the importance of European teamwork, children will indirectly reap the benefits in terms of a greater understanding of other cultures and traditions. The benefits of international co-operation has already been seen in the numerous projects that are now underway using electronic network links. Wouldn't this represent a first step at the primary school to realise one of the fundamental goals of the European Union - to promote unity and collaboration between Member States?

International exchanges on the integration of IT in primary schools could provide a secondary advantage, by awakening the interest of teachers in speaking a foreign language. Teachers represent a role model for the children they teach, and have an important influence on their pupils' attitude to foreign language learning. It has been noted throughout this study that foreign language learning is almost non-existent at the primary school level. If every European is to be fluent in at least two foreign languages,[12] every step should be taken to promote co-operation between teachers in Europe.

2) The Ampère Group's second recommendation is that a major effort be made in the field of teacher training. Initial training courses should:

• provide every trainee teacher with a wide experience **in the use of IT as a learning instrument**. Like all learners, teachers reproduce the role models of those who teach them. If they are to use IT in their own teaching, they must be given the opportunity to appreciate its value in their own learning experiences. Teaching them about IT serves no purpose at all, a "learning through doing" approach should be adopted.

• lead trainee teachers to use **an active research method** while they are learning to teach. Progress is taking place at a momentous rate, the tools of today will perhaps become obsolete tomorrow. Consequently teachers must be encouraged to develop the skills which, as for their pupils, will enable them to seek their own knowledge and make their own cognitive associations if they are to cope with the changes taking place around them.

---

12. European Commission, *Livre blanc sur l'education et la formation*, Brussels, European Commission, 1995, p. 49

• lead trainee teachers to discover the **pedagogical approaches and organisational methods** which will enable them to successfully incorporate IT in their classrooms.

• free them from the constraints of an outmoded curriculum to develop **a cross-curricular approach** enabling them to take full advantages of the rich learning environment that IT offers.

• develop an awareness of the importance of **adapting teaching style to the individual learning rhythms of pupils** and initiate teachers in the methods that can be used to individualise teaching.

• develop the **strategies of communication, social relations and teamwork** necessary to promote rich pupil/teacher, pupil/pupil interactions in class, and to enrich their own learning environment with other staff members. Only if a teacher is capable of communicating freely with his pupils will he be able to discard the role of "master" in a teacher-directed environment, to become guide, counsellor and mentor in a pupil-directed environment where every child can develop his full capacities as an autonomous lifelong learner.

• develop **new, more meaningful assessment methods** that will lead each learner to assess his progress in terms of his own learning aptitudes and objectives.

• **open up the learning environment at teachers college** through contact with trainee teachers in other European Member States and awaken them to the importance of continually updating their knowledge through on-line professional services and professional literature. It is alarming to see that, although no self-respecting medical practitioner ignores the importance of keeping up to date with changes in the medical world, teachers who hold the future of our children in their hands rarely receive professional documentation. In schools, it would be the role of the IT co-ordinator to see that every staff member has access to such material.

In-service courses should focus on the same areas as initial teacher training courses. The IT co-ordinator should be made responsible for informing teachers of courses available.

3) Thirdly, we strongly recommend that the European Union make every effort to see that all classes in every nation be equipped with at least two or three computers per class.

The observations included in this report underline the importance of interaction between pupils when IT is incorporated in the learning process. One computer per child would deprive learners of the enriching interactions that contribute to the value of the computer as a teaching/learning medium. This factor should not be overlooked. The computer should become an integral part of classroom equipment, to help the teacher extend his potential teaching capacity and to free him from as many tasks as possible if he is to assume a new role in the individualised learning process of his pupils.

The **hardware industry should be encouraged to play their part** in equipping schools by constructing equipment truly adapted to the needs of young learners, providing ongoing advice and maintenance to the schools they equip and offering favourable financial conditions for updating school equipment. Tax incentives could be introduced to accelerate efforts in this domain. In Portugal, the purchase of a computer for home use is a tax deduction. This idea could be extended to companies wishing to invest in the intellectual capital of our future workforce. **The telecommunications industry also has a role to play**, and has already done so in many countries, in aiding all schools to have at least one electronic network connection, with a minimum charge for connection with other schools and educational services.

*

* *

The decision made by heads of state at the summit meeting held in Florence in June, 1996, to open the European multimedia industry to the world of education offers a wonderful opportunity that must be seized upon if we are to assist teachers in their Art of Teaching and aid them to develop in our children a fundamental strategy: the "Research Reasoning Method"[13]. Children will hence be better equipped to face the demands of a society governed by competition, globalisation of markets and professions, and a growing complexity in the rules of decision-making.

When confronted with these implacable vectors of development, coming generations will perhaps be more capable of applying their intelligence in **situations** and in **relations** when they are making decisions. It is only in this way that the essential driving forces in the development of nations

"Competition - Co-operation - Nucleation"[14]

can function naturally, "leaving man the time not just to create robots, but to create children in his own image"[15].

---

13. Deberghes D., De la vie à l'école, à l'école de la vie, in La Formation en Europe, *Annales des Mines*, Paris, 1993

14. Danzin D., *La Croissance Autrement*, Paris, L'Institut de l'Energie, 1993

15. Deberghes D., *Le Temps Partagé*, Paris, Agence de l'Informatique, Ministère de l'Industrie, 1986

Bibliography

ALBEDA W., Vers de nouvelles responsibilités des pouvoirs publiques, in *Annales des Mines*, Paris, 1993

BALL C., Learning Pays, Interim Report, in the *RSA Journal*, April 1991

BAUDÉ J., Rapports d'activités et orientations pour 1995-96, in *La Revue de l'association EPI*, December 1995, N°80

BIBEAU R., Attention! Passage étroit - "Autoroute pédagogique", in *La revue de l'association EPI*, Paris, September 1995

CARNEVALE A.P., Skill and the New Economy, in *Gestion 2000*, 1992, N°4

CERI, *Information Technologies and Basic Learning*, Paris, OECD, 1987

COCHINAUX, P., de Woot, P., *Moving Towards a Learning Society*, Louvain, CRE-ERT, 1995

COHEN R., *Quand l'Ordinateur Parle*, Paris, PUF, 1992

COUNCIL OF EUROPE, A Role for Information Technology in Practical Science, in the Final Report of the 45th European Teachers' Seminar, *Information Technology in Science Education*, Council of Europe, 1989

COUNCIL FOR CULTURAL CO-OPERATION: School Education Division, *Innovation in Primary Education*, Strasbourg, Council of Europe, 1988

COUNCIL OF EUROPE GROUP REPORT, The Role of Computers for Modelling in Science Education, in the Final Report of the 45th European Teachers' Seminar, *Information Technology in Science Education*, Council of Europe, 1989

COX M.J., JOHNSON D.C., *The ImpacT Report*, London, King's College, 1993

DALY F., *CD-ROM in Education*, U.K., NCET, 1995

DANZIN D., *La Croissance Autrement*, Paris, L'Institut de l'Energie, 1993

DA PONTE J.P., *MINERVA project - Introducing NIT in Education*, DEPGEF, Portugal, 1994

DE LANDSHEERE V., *L'Education et la Formation*, France, PUF, 1992

DE LANDSHEERE G., *L'illetrisme, une menace pour les individus et l'économie du pays*, to be published

DEBERGHES D., De la vie à l'école à l'école de la vie, in *La Formation en Europe*, Annales des Mines, Paris, 1993

DEBERGHES D., *La Formation aux Technologies de l'Information et de la Communication en Europe et la Subsidiarité* (AFCET International Congress, Versailles, 1993)

DEBERGHES D., La Formation en Europe in *Annales des Mines*, Paris, 1993

DEBERGHES D., *Le Temps Partagé*, Paris, Agence de l'Informatique, Ministère de l'Industrie, 1986

DEBERGHES D., *L'information dans l'économie européenne*, Paris, Annales des Mines, 1992

DEBERGHES D., *L'information électronique, vecteur de croissance ou de crise, de la révolution Gutenberg à la révolution Shannon,* Luxembourg, C.C.E. XIII, 1993

DEBERGHES D., *Télécommunication, information, technologies*, Paris, Annales des Mines, 1993

DELACOTE G., *Savoir apprendre: les nouvelles méthodes*, Paris, UNESCO Editions Odile Jacob, 1996

DELORS J., *L'éducation - un trésor est caché dedans*, Paris, UNESCO/Editions Odile Jacob, 1996

DEWEY J., *Democracy and Education,* New York, The Macmillan Company, 1916

DONALDSON M., *Children's Minds,* Glasgow, Fontana Press, 1978

ELSTGEEST J., HARLEN W., *UNESCO sourcebook for science in the primary school*, Paris, UNESCO, 1992

EPI, Dossier de Presse, in *La revue de l'association EPI,* Paris, September 1995

EUROPEAN COMMISSION, Lifelong Learning, in issue 4 of *Le Magazine for Education, Training and Youth in Europe*, Brussels, European Commission, 1995

EUROPEAN COMMISSION, *Livre blanc sur l'éducation et la formation*, Brussels, European Commission, 1995,

EURYDICE, *Key data on Education in the EU - 1994, European Commission (Education, Training and Youth),* Brussels, European Commission, 1995

EURYDICE, *Key data on Education in the EU - 1995, European Commission (Education, Training and Youth),* Brussels, European Commission, 1996

FEURZEIG W., Algebra Slaves and Agents in a LOGO-based Mathematics Curriculum, *Instructional Science,* 14, 1986

FINNISH MINISTRY OF EDUCATION, *Education, Training and Research in the Information Society: A National Strategy*, Helsinki, Ministry of Education, 1995

FORDHAM P., *L'éducation pour tous: une vision élargie*, Paris, UNESCO, 1994

GRETSCH G., *TEO - Développement et evaluation d'un traitement de texte orale,* Luxembourg, Ministère de l'Education Nationale, 1994

HAGGIS S., *L'éducation pour tous : les objectifs et le contexte*, Paris, UNESCO, 1993

HART B., HOLT G., FLETCHER C., Tyldesley A., *Extending Horizons*, U.K., NCET, 1994

ISAKSSON T., *Children of the Future*, (unpublished), Sweden, 1995

LATREILLE A., AMPERE A-M.: L'homme, la pensée, l'influence, dans *Cahiers d'Histoire,* Polymieux, France, Ed. Ste A-M. Ampère, 1975

LEWIS R., The Contribution of Information Technologies to Learning, in the Final Report of the 45th European Teachers' Seminar, *Information Technology in Science Education*, Council of Europe, 1989

MARBEAU V., Les perpectives offertes par l'informatique et les technologies de la communication, in *La Revue de l'association EPI*, Paris, EPI, 1995, N°79

MC CORMICK L., *The Art of Teaching Writing*, Heinemann, Portsmouth, 1994

MERZENICH MM, JENKINS WM, JOHNSTON P, SCHREINER C, MILLER SL, TALLAL P,: Temporal processing deficits of language-learning impaired children ameliorated by training, in *Science*, USA, 5th Jan. 1996, N° 271

MINISTER OF CULTURAL AFFAIRS, *Technologies nouvelles dans le domaine de l'information et communication à l'école - concept cadre*, Dusseldorf, Minister of Cultural Affairs of North-Westphalie Rheinland, 1985

MINISTRY OF EDUCATION, *Education, Training and Research in the Information Society - a national strategy*, Helsinki, Ministry of Education, 1995

MITTERRAND F., *Discours du 150ᵉ anniversaire de la mort d'A-M. AMPERE*, La Villette, Paris, 1986

NASH J.M., Zooming in on Dyslexia, in *Time International*, 26 January, 1996

NCET, *CD-ROM in Education*, UK, NCET, 1995

NCET, *Getting started with Information Handling*, U.K., NCET, 1994

NCET, *Integrated Learning Systems - a report on the pilot evaluation of ILS in the UK*, Coventry, NCET, 1994

NCET, *Libraries of the future*, as yet unpublished report, Coventry, 1995

NCET, *Primary Science Investigations with IT*, U.K., NCET, 1994

OECD, DEPGEF, *Report of the MINERVA Project Evaluators*, Lisbon, Ministry of Education, 1994

OGBORN J., The Role of Modelling in Science Education, in the Final Report of the 45th European Teachers' Seminar, *Information Technology in Science Education*, Council of Europe, 1989

PANTZAR E., POHJOLAINEN S., RUOKAMO-SAARI H., VITELI J., *Theoretical Foundations and Applications of Modern Learning Environments*, Finland, Tampereen yliopisto, 1995

PAPERT S., *The Children's Machine: Rethinking School in the Age of the Computer*, New York, Harvester/Wheatsheaf, 1993

PELGRUM W.J., PLOMP T., *The IEA Study of Computers in Education*, U.K., Pergamon Press, 1993

PLAISANCE E., VERGNAUD G., *Les sciences de l'education*, Paris, La découverte, 1993

ROUSSEAU, J-J., *Du Contrat Social*, extract from the Encyclopaedia Brittanica

RUSS J., *Histoire de la Philosophie*, Paris, Armand Colin, 1993

SÉGARD N. (Minister of Telecommunications), *Technologies et Société: Rapport au Premier Ministre*, Paris, La Documentation Française, 1985

SIRCHIA G., Schola Trapani Sicile, *Schola Mutimediale*, Italy, Editions RAI, 1993

UNESCO, Proceedings of a European Workshop, Université of Twente, *Information technologies in teacher education*, Paris, UNESCO, 1995

UNESCO, *World education report - 1995*, Paris, UNESCO, 1995

WINDHAM D., *L'éducation pour tous : les conditions requises*, Paris, UNESCO, 1994

WOOD D., *How Children Learn and Think*, Oxford, UK, Blackwell, 1988

ANNEX I
"BACKGROUND" GRIDS

(in order of presentation throughout book)

GRID N° 1

ID/COUNTRY:	I - 1
NAME OF PROJECT:	Italy 8 schools in area of Bologna
DURATION:	1990-1996
OBJECT:	An IT co-ordinator was appointed to look after 8 schools in the Bologna area, to: - train teachers in technical & pedagogical aspects of computer use in primary education - work with teachers in class for an initial period - run workshops for specific applications
PROJECT DESCRIPTION:	A laboratory containing five IBM-compatible (80386 and 80486) computers was set up in each of the 8 schools, funded by local communities & fund-raising events organised by parents. Laboratories are linked by e-mail with a total of 30 schools in the area. Projects (on environment, search for pen pals) have been run through electronic links with schools in England, Canada, Australia & other parts of Italy
ORGANISATION:	The IT co-ordinator spends time in each of the 8 schools, training & encouraging teachers to set up their own projects. He also develops software to meet the needs of chn with learning difficulties and physical handicaps
TEACHER TRAINING:	Originally a primary teacher, this IT co-ordinator followed a course run by the Minister of Education to promote the use of IT in education. At present seconded to the Ministry, he runs his own projects in all 8 schools, in which almost all teachers have taken part in basic IT courses & refresher courses in all subject areas, e.g. the use of logic in mathematical activities
USER'S COMMENTS:	"IT is especially useful for children with problems of logic, I make my own puzzles for them which are now being used by 13 schools. IT helps all children learn more quickly & easily, they have teacher + IT to help them." He stresses the need for someone to test products to relieve teachers of this responsibility - "teachers must think of everything, but they should be freed to concentrate on pedagogical aspects"
FUNDING:	Laboratories were funded by local communities and a grant from the Ministry of Education
FORMAL EVALUATION:	The project was presented at a conference "Scuola 2.1" organised by the Department of Studies in Bologna and the Emilia Romagna region
FURTHER READING:	A number of software programs, worksheets and users' manuals are available from the IT co-ordinator, Mr Walter Casamenti. For details on QUANTOFA project: Proceedings from Scuola 2.1 conference, page 7
USEFUL ADDRESSES:	Walter Casamenti, via Calanco, 166/C, 40014 Crevalcore (Bologna) Italy QUANTOFA distributed by Flash Computers, via Crevalcore, 5/c 40017 S.G. in Persiceto (Bologna), Italy - fax 39-51 825250

GRID N° 2

ID/COUNTRY:	1- UK
NAME OF PROJECT:	UK - Integrated Learning Systems
DURATION:	Phase 1: 01/94 - 07/94, level KS2 and KS3 in 4 UK schools; Phase 2: 01/95 - 07/95, level KS1,2 & 3 in 8 UK schools
OBJECT:	To produce learning gains in basic skills (mathematics, reading, language skills); to improve learning attitude, and consequently motivation; to cater to the needs of underachievers through the use of individualised programs. Teacher assigns entry level, children work upward through levels in all strands, a success rate is attributed per strand per session
PROJECT DESCRIPTION:	Project uses desktop multimedia computers connected to a powerful server on an Ethernet-type configuration (80 486 DX, 16 Mb RAM, 1 Gb storage capacity) running "Success Maker" software incorporating a management system and IPM (initial placement modules); overall performance assessment, diagnostic modules and written worksheets included
ORGANISATION:	3 adjoining classrooms (30 students per class) in an open-planning area with raised computer area in centre. Participating children, chosen at random, are rostered for 1/2 hour sessions throughout the day
TEACHER TRAINING:	Phase 1: 1-week residential course for 2 or 3 key staff members; Phase 2: 3-5 day residential (organised by NCET & software supplier) on ILS related issues, curriculum content & work levels: management system, IP techniques & feed-back, awareness of differences between American & British system. Participants exchange addresses to continue to share experience & resolve problems
USER'S COMMENTS:	Noticeable improvement in behaviour of underachievers. System provides extension work that can be used by ILS-experienced teachers with whole class. Reporting system can be developed to diagnose class achievement. "Efficient, convenient work program with useful feedback for conscientious learners" "A European product seems desirable" "Could be expanded to other subjects"
FUNDING:	Departments of Education for England, Scotland & Wales
FORMAL EVALUATION:	NCET (cf Further Reading)
FURTHER READING:	NCET, Integrated Learning Systems - A report of the pilot evaluation of ILS in the UK, Coventry, NCET, 1994;
USEFUL ADDRESSES:	NCET (National Council for Educational Technology), Milburn Hill Road, Science Park, Coventry CV4 7JJ, UK Tel: 01203 416994 Software Supplier: Dr John de Witt, 8680 Scenic H/way, Unit 15, Pensacola FL32514, USA Fax/phone: 904 476 696

GRID N° 3

ID/COUNTRY:	I 2
NAME OF PROJECT:	Italy, Elementary school, Correggio - RE
DURATION:	Phase 1 (11/93-6/94) & 2 (11/94-6/95)- Livello Elementary School, grades 1-5 (10 classes); Phase 3 (10/95-6/96) - grade 3 (2 classes)
OBJECT:	- familiarise pupils with the concept of symbols, messages, meanings, instructions, information organised to initiate them in the structure of the language - lead the child to perceive the use of natural language, then progressively, formalised language - develop capacity to predict, organise operations in problem solving - use computer to organise their own resources & time, in a climate of collaboration
PROJECT DESCRIPTION:	A laboratory with 7 computers (MS-DOS) and 2 printers linked in a network organisation. Software: LOGOWRITER, which combines LOGO graphics, text, animations with 4 turtles & sounds. This is a primary school project for use of computer as a cross-curricular tool
ORGANISATION:	Pupils are divided into two groups, one working in lab. with computer teacher, the other in class working with subject teacher on complementary activities: summarising, developing concepts, writing up their own explanations or designing other activities
TEACHER TRAINING:	Teachers in lab. were given training courses from 1988 onwards; annual in-service courses are provided by CRIN in this region to introduce teachers to the language, organisational methods for group work, didactical approaches and to allow them to learn from the previous experiences of CRIN
USER'S COMMENTS:	The program enables the teacher to structure a MICROWORLD, a specific learning environment adapted to the competencies of children from 6 - 11 yrs in diverse subject areas. MAGICTURTLE: topological orientation for chn at early levels; TER: (geometrical) STORY-GAMES: (linguistic) for grade 2 upwards; LAB (geometric or geographical) and LOGOIT (geometrical/logic) for chn in middle grades
FUNDING:	Community of CORREGGIO: provision of the laboratory Minister of Public Education: supplied IT co-ordinator for phases 1 & 2 Community of REGGIO-EMILIA CRIN (Centre for Research in Informatics): teacher training. By phase 3, tchrs had sufficiently progressed to be able to conduct the experiments in the 2 classes alone.
FORMAL EVALUATION:	No formal assessment has been carried out
FURTHER READING:	Documents relevant to LOGOWRITER & MICROWORLD (containing pedagogical material) are available from author.
USEFUL ADDRESSES:	SCUOLA Elementare "Cantona" - via Newton,1 - 42015 Correggio (RE) CRIN - Assessorato P.1., Via G da Castello, Commune de Reggio Emilia LOGO Computer System - 3300 Cote Vertu Rd, Suite 201- Montreal, Quebec - Canad

GRID N° 4

ID/COUNTRY:	I-F
NAME OF PROJECT:	France - Smalltalk, un jeu d'enfant - object-oriented programming
DURATION:	Project introduced by Isabelle Borne on MICRO-SMALLTALK in LE-LISP in 1985. Later versions developed on Macintosh, trial runs in class continue through 1995 & 1996
OBJECT:	To initiate 8-10 yr olds in IT through use of interactive object-oriented programming tools to: 1/ create "wallpapers" using objects provided on menu or geometric shapes with basic geometrical concepts (translation, symmetry, rotation...) 2/ conjugate verbs to develop understanding of tense, mode, but also to develop conceptual understanding of verb patterns
PROJECT DESCRIPTION:	Developed by I. Borne, R. Durand & teacher trainer C. Girardot, the pilot class (CM2) is in a school attached to teacher training college. One computer & colour printer was installed in class during project by Macintosh. Jan & Feb 95: whole class discovered basic features & functions of computer & Smalltalk; March - June: work on verb conjugation & step-by-step "programming" to make each wallpaper type
ORGANISATION:	Class (27 children) divided into 9 groups of 3, each group spent 4 x 1/2 to 3/4 hour sessions on computer. Screen prints presented to whole class on overhead projector during "global" teaching sessions enabling children to exchange ideas & discoveries
TEACHER TRAINING:	Formal training on use of Smalltalk has not yet begun, Mrs Girardot is present in class with teacher. She runs initial training & further training sessions (during which trainee teachers replace class teacher for up to 3 months) to advise on how to use IT in creation of teaching aids & as a teaching tool (UIFM-Creteil)
USER'S COMMENTS:	"Innovative teachers have always found the means to use "multimedia" in class to give children first-hand learning experiences, computing just provides an easier, faster, more powerful tool to improve teaching style. It is essential that we develop the innovative capacity in trainee teachers, & to give them hands-on experience of IT leading them to realise by themselves the wealth of resources it offers."
FUNDING:	All those concerned in this project contribute their own leisure time & use their own equipment, except for loan of material by Macintosh
FORMAL EVALUATION:	Continued assessment by above-mentioned project developers, who have produced a number of reports on the subject.
FURTHER READING:	Several books have been written by Adele Goldberg et al., Xerox Palo Alto Research Center, USA. A number of articles and conference presentations by I. Borne and C. Girardot are available
USEFUL ADDRESSES:	I. Borne, Ecole des Mines de Nantes, 4 rue Alfred Kastler, La Chantrerie, 44070 Nantes CEDEX 03 C. Girardot, PIUFM, l'UFM de Paris, 10 rue Molitor, 75016 PARIS R. Durand, Université, Paris VI, 4 place Jussieu, 75252 PARIS

GRID N° 5

ID/COUNTRY:	I-LUX
NAME OF PROJECT:	Luxembourg - TEO (oral word processing)
DURATION:	Jan-July 93 - development of software; Sep-Dec 93 - trial runs in 3 classes, production of brochure; Jan-July 94 - perfection of software, pedagogical methods, use in 6 classes
OBJECT:	To implement a means by which peer group learning, a fundamental aspect in 2nd language development, could be used to advantage. Acquaint chn with computer use, and develop greater autonomy & control in learning process
PROJECT DESCRIPTION:	TEO consists of a blank screen, a simplified menu bar, & icons at bottom of screen which, when activated, record a spoken sentence. Icons are placed in required order on screen to tell a story. Chn thus become aware of their own production & begin to permanently assess it; through auto-evaluation they become actively involved in learning process; active listening skills are also developed
ORGANISATION:	Introduced into primary schools in 3 stages, software & pedagogical aspects assessed by questionnaire & interview. Stories produced on TEO have been compiled on CD. Video cassettes on use of TEO are available (parent information etc.)
TEACHER TRAINING:	Teachers have taken an active part in development process of software & pedagogical material. Materials available to teachers (written report, brochure: "Initiation for Beginners", "aide-memoire" to facilitate use in class, CD of typical stories produced, video cassette showing how software is used) enable practising teachers to follow an auto-training & can be used in initial training
USER'S COMMENTS:	"Provides pupils with a powerful tool to reflect upon their own output"; "Encourages active learning of oral language through collaboration, elaboration, correction, exchange of ideas; develops pupils' autonomy & sense of responsibility"; "Could be extended to practice native language, or for use at any level from pre-school to adult"
FUNDING:	R & D project presented by SCRIPT (Coordination & Research Service for Pedagogical & Technical Innovation) & ISERP (Institute for Superior Studies & Pedagogical Research - teachers' college). Software produced by CRP-HT (Henri Tudor Centre for Public Research). Assistance in production & distribution of CD & video cassette from CTE (Centre for Technology in Education)
FORMAL EVALUATION:	SCRIPT, ISERP, CRP-HT and CTE, by means of questionnaire & interviews. Given limited number of schools in this tiny country, on-going improvements are being made on recommendations of users
FURTHER READING:	Above-mentioned brochure, written report, etc. available from SCRIPT; Gérard GRETSCH, "TEO - development & assessment of an oral text processor", , National Education Ministry, Luxembourg, 1995 (available only in French)
USEFUL ADDRESSES:	SCRIPT, National Education Ministry, 29 rue Aldringen, L-2926 LUXEMBOURG; Tel: 352-4785211

GRID N° 6

ID/COUNTRY:	2-LUX
NAME OF PROJECT:	Luxembourg "Open classroom", 11-12 year-olds
DURATION:	An on-going project, first computers were installed in this school in 1993. Since then more computers have been bought with funds from local community
OBJECT:	To develop autonomous learning & encourage group work: screen is "public", all children feel free to input ideas on the work of others. Class teacher, Mr Fiermonte, motivated by the open-type classroom - "TVIND" - that exists in Nordic countries, is convinced that all children are able to learn by themselves, it is the context that leads them to learn
PROJECT DESCRIPTION:	Classroom is equipped with 5 computers & a telephone available to children (e.g. to contact an editor or author for a book revue), and to transmit data to other schools in France & Canada working on joint weekly newsletter. A Mac Quick Time is used to take photos & scan images, teacher considers the use of images important in today's "media" society. Chn spend day working on their projects, few real "classes" take place
ORGANISATION:	Children choose their own group, their own projects, telephone any organisations necessary for information & go to visit factories etc. to consolidate data & set up exhibitions for class & school. Daily newspapers are delivered to class & used judiciously
TEACHER TRAINING:	Initial training at ISERP, close collaboration with SCRIPT & active participation in APTICE (Association pour la Promotion des Technologies de l'Information et de la Communication à l'Ecole) which works towards implementation of IT in primary education in Luxembourg. Mr Fiermonte considers teacher training should open up teacher's eyes just as school does for children
USER'S COMMENTS:	"Before drawing up annual program, the teacher must reflect on the socio-cultural environment. IT is a socio-cultural factor and school must develop life-long attitudes that correspond to the needs of a democratic society." "We don't use CD-ROM - its too easy and too perfect"
FUNDING:	Equipment in the primary education sector in Luxembourg is funded by the local community and by fund-raising activities for special needs (e.g. Mac Quick Image). Telephone costs are covered by school budget. The APTICE is a non-profit-making organisation for which teachers work benevolently to assess & develop projects
FORMAL EVALUATION:	No formal evaluation organised. Mr Fiermonte works with the same class for two years, results in formal "end of primary education" exam are no better or no worse than those of pupils following a traditional cursus (though other teachers in school admit that the class observed was considered as being particularly "difficult" in preceding years).
FURTHER READING:	
USEFUL ADDRESSES:	APTICE a.s.b.l., 20 rue de l'Ecole, L-3233 Bettembourg, LUXEMBOURG SCRIPT, National Education Ministry, 29 rue Aldringen, L-2926 LUXEMBOURG

GRID N° 7

ID/COUNTRY:	Portugal
NAME OF PROJECT:	"Imagination in my school"
DURATION:	2 years
OBJECT:	- enrich the learning environment - motivate chn by developing sense of experimentation and team spirit - improve quality of teaching by providing chn with real life tools - develop strategies of independent lifelong learning - promote interest in schoolwork through telematics
PROJECT DESCRIPTION:	4 classes share resource centre equipped with 4 computers and telematic link, to work on cross-curricular projects chosen by children
ORGANISATION:	Each class uses centre for one full day per week. 12 year-olds have access to computers every day
TEACHER TRAINING:	5 years training in IT use in Ecole Supérieure (Higher teacher studies); 6 years in telematic training, one course per week; trains colleagues involved in project (cascade model)
USER'S COMMENTS:	Class teachers are responsible for use of IT with their class now that their training has been completed. There is no set work program for IT use, each teacher chooses the activities to develop with his class
FUNDING:	Institute of Innovation in Education, Lisbon; Municipality of Sintra; Junta de Freguesia de Algueirao - Mem Martins
FORMAL EVALUATION:	Ongoing evaluation
FURTHER READING:	School newspaper, "O despertar das crianças"
USEFUL ADDRESSES:	Escola Piloto, Rua de Macau, 2725 Mem Martins, PORTUGAL Instituto de Inovaçao Educacional, Rua Artilharia Um, 105, 1000 Lisboa, PORTUGAL

GRID N° 8

ID/COUNTRY:	5-UK
NAME OF PROJECT:	UK - CD-ROM
DURATION:	Phase 1: 1994 - 2,300 schools equipped; total budget £4.5m Phase 2: 1995 - extended to 5,000 schools; total budget £5m
OBJECT:	Introduce interactive multimedia into primary education to cater to the wide abilities in a class & provide a wealth of resource material for non-specialist primary teachers
PROJECT DESCRIPTION:	Participating schools were provided with one multimedia platform & 6 CD titles. One year later, 24% of schools had bought more computers, all had bought more CD-ROM titles. Most schools now also use their computer for other activities
ORGANISATION:	NCET assessed performance of 20 hardware systems & 500 titles, producing a detailed catalogue for teacher use. A field officer was appointed to visit schools & develop support material to help teachers integrate CD-ROM into their program of work
TEACHER TRAINING:	All teachers concerned followed a training course to learn how to use computer for their personal work, gain confidence in IT use & thus encourage its introduction into class, become awakened to the possibilities it offers
USER'S COMMENTS:	Would like to have an overview chart of each CD-ROM to see curriculum relevance of topics covered and worksheet resources to facilitate use of encyclopaedias both at machine and before and after lesson. Often encounter sound problems which hinder effective use
FUNDING:	National Department of Education (Great Britain)
FORMAL EVALUATION:	Ongoing evaluation of CD-ROM titles for quality & curriculum-relevance by NCET, results brought to teachers in a yearly catalogue in which top-quality products are attributed a seal of approval
FURTHER READING:	NCET, CD-ROM in Education, Coventry, NCET, 1995 for CD-ROM catalogue and project description
USEFUL ADDRESSES:	NCET (National Council for Educational Technology) Milburn Hill Rd, Science Park, Coventry CV47JJ, U.K.

GRID N° 9

ID/COUNTRY:	3-UK
NAME OF PROJECT:	UK - BBC/NCET Internet project (Potters Green)
DURATION:	6 months, late 1994 to mid 1995
OBJECT:	Test use of Internet in tchng & learning to: obtain information on a wide range of subjects, encourage chn to learn independently & share information with class, enhance cross-curricular skills of information retrieval, handling & presentation, discern relevant importance of lesson-planning & teacher development, assess value of e-mail & information access via graphical browser, evaluate content suitability
PROJECT DESCRIPTION:	In Jan 1994, NCET became advisory partner to BBC Education in development of BBC Networking Club to provide connectivity to Internet & carry BBC resources. Most participating schools are equipped with PC 486 with 14,400 baud modem & printer. Voluntary workers (mothers) play an important role in supervising chn working in groups, since activity takes place wherever phone point exists
ORGANISATION:	Part of a pilot scheme (270 centres, including 20 primary & secondary schools) set up to trial the BBCNC Auntielink, in aim of developing electronic communication applications suitable for use in schools. Questionnaires & e-mail used for feedback
TEACHER TRAINING:	Self-help & "cascade" models most prevalent for teachers (and children) involved in pilot project. Definite need felt for on- & off-line courses with tutor support to avoid widening gap between users & non-users. Pilot highlighted potential for distance learning, both in training itself & in advertising courses available
USER'S COMMENTS:	One Technology College suggests linking home & school & used pilot as first stage in assessing how this could work as a means of changing future ways of learning. Teachers expressed a need for a trusted body such as NCET or BBC to provide mediated information services. E-mail is seen as a means of promoting cultural understanding & as being applicable to all subject areas
FUNDING:	NCET; British Library Research & Development Department; Department of Education, Northern Ireland; subsidised access to Business Briefing service provided by Reuters
FORMAL EVALUATION:	For the moment, anecdotal rather than hard evidence, but feedback indicates considerable learning gains and a changing role for teachers & librarians (see Bibliography: "Libraries of the Future"). Results highlight questions & issues to be examined in Phase 2 (May 1995 - April 1996)
FURTHER READING:	As yet, results of project have not been published. See "Libraries of the Future" in Bibliography
USEFUL ADDRESSES:	NCET, Milburn Hill Road, Science Park, Coventry CV4 7JJ, UK. Tel: 44-1203 416994 Judith Banbury, BBC Networking Club, Room 401, Sulgrave House, Woodger Road, London W12 8QT, UK. Tel: 44-181 576 7799

GRID N° 10

ID/COUNTRY:	1-B
NAME OF PROJECT:	Belgium - Interactive multimedia projects
DURATION:	Project began 3 yrs ago, has since been developed in a total of 3 schools in the following subjects: history, geography, science, religion, music, technology, French
OBJECT:	Aims: to introduce children to use of IT to create interactive multimedia projects that can be used as teaching software for other classes; to develop awareness of importance of sound, image & interactivity to communicate ideas; to develop tree-type non-linear organisation for interactive presentation of ideas
PROJECT DESCRIPTION:	Project developed by Mr Francis LAGAE & Mme Eliane JACQUES (CREADIM), both retired voluntary workers seeking a means of helping today's generation confront challenges presented by new technology. They presented their idea to IBM, who set up the computer laboratory in the Basse-Wavre school. They have developed similar projects at Bierges & Heverlee, in Belgium
ORGANISATION:	Children separate class project into complementary modules, decide on skeleton schema necessary (input by Mr LAGAE & Mme HALLOT out of school hours because of limited duration of course), carry out research to find text & images, then input data
TEACHER TRAINING:	Mr LAGAE & Mme JACQUES spend a great amount of time training interested teachers (not paid for the extra tasks they take on), helping choose modules & developing projects in class, drawing up skeleton schema out of school hours, raising funds for equipment, promoting the concept to other schools (Switzerland is interested in project), staying in liaison with sponsors (IBM)
USER'S COMMENTS:	Mme Hallot : "Takes up a lot of free time but is worth it when we see the motivation of even (or most particularly) the poorer students. When children handle their own sound, text & image, they develop a new understanding of the strategies of the media... the module is far too short and should become a subject in its own right rather than being squeezed into science
FUNDING:	Sponsorship from IBM (supply of machines) CREADIM is a non-profit making organisation, Mr LAGAE & Mme JACQUES work benevolently, carry out all teacher training and raise necessary funds to add to equipment when necessary
FORMAL EVALUATION:	None as yet, though other schools (in Belgium & abroad) are making contact with CREADIM to set up similar projects with their pupils. IBM has closely followed project (see Further reading)
FURTHER READING:	IBM INFORMATIONS - October 1994: Enseignement: une interactivé, peut en cacher une autre (Teaching: one type of interactivity may hide another)
USEFUL ADDRESSES:	Francis LAGAE, Ernest Claeslaan, 8 - B-3080 Tervuren, Tel: (322) 7673796; Fax: Mme Eliane JACQUES, route de l'Etat, 351 - B-1380 Lasne-Maransart, Tel: (322) 6333428 Mme Michelle Hallot (class teacher), rue Joseph Joppart, 30 - B-1300 Wavre

GRID N° 11

ID/COUNTRY:	4 - UK
NAME OF PROJECT:	Northamptonshire Distance In-Service Training
DURATION:	Sept 94 - July 95
OBJECT:	- To investigate new professional training opportunities for tchrs (science has been identified as area of new national curriculum where most training is needed) - Reduce costs of training in isolated country areas.
PROJECT DESCRIPTION:	Grendon primary has a staff of 3 teachers (two part-time) & 75 pupils. The overall project attempts to overcome economic difficulties & traditional limits that exist for a total 450 pupils & 24 teachers (the "cluster")
ORGANISATION:	A project based on network information technology providing interactive access to learning materials, expert advice (from NIAS - Northamptonshire Inspection & Advisory Service), tutorial & peer support. Programs provided by Network Learning Ltd
TEACHER TRAINING:	A CD-ROM based on existing text-based INSET materials adapted to take full advantage of multimedia is used to examine how this model of INSET delivery might prove to be more cost-effective than traditional training models, change teachers' behaviour & improve pupils' learning more effectively than traditional methods & be particularly relevant to needs of small rural schools
USER'S COMMENTS:	Mrs Rivers (head teacher/teacher): "At first I was worried about time needed for training in system use; e-mail introduced to reduce telephone costs & because written information system proved more efficient for minutes & organisation of meetings, questions & answers on curriculum-planning issues. Objective was teacher training, outcome is an invaluable means of communication."
FUNDING:	£100,000 provided by Dept of Education; Network Learning Ltd & NIAS are contributing staff, materials & equipment. The Wellcome Foundation Ltd. is funding some of tchr training & support materials
FORMAL EVALUATION:	Independent evaluation, funded by Dept of Ed. & Rural Development Commission & managed by NCET & Leicester University School of Education, will determine degree to which this new model of distance supported INSET is successful against a number of criteria
FURTHER READING:	As yet not available
USEFUL ADDRESSES:	NIAS - Mike Rumble, General Ed. Inspector, PO Box 216, John Dryden House, 8-10 The Lakes, Northampton NN4 7DD Network Learning Ltd. - Tony Eldridge, 4 Oak Tree Copse, Tilehurst, Reading, Berkshire RG3 6P

ANNEX II
LIST OF THOSE CONSULTED
OR INTERVIEWED

AVIS P., NCET, *Milburn Hill Road, Science Park, Coventry CV4 7JJ UK.*

BELL M., NCET, *Milburn Hill Road, Science Park, Coventry CV4 7JJ UK.*

BÉNARD Da Costa A-M., *Instit. de Inovaçao Educacional, P-1000 Lisbon, Portugal.*

BLAMIRE R., NCET, *Milburn Hill Road, Science Park, Coventry CV4 7JJ UK.*

BROWN J., NCET, *Milburn Hill Road, Science Park, Coventry CV4 7JJ UK.*

CATALOA Alves C., *Instit. de Inovaçao Educacional, P-1000 Lisbon, Portugal.*

CASAMENTI W., *Via Calanco 166/C, Crevalcore, I-40014, Italy.*

DALY F., NCET, *Milburn Hill Road, Science Park, Coventry CV4 7JJ UK.*

DANBY M., NCET, *Milburn Hill Road, Science Park, Coventry CV4 7JJ UK.*

DEBERNARDI V., *CRIN - Via Guido da Castello 12, Re, Italy.*

de GOEI B., PRINT, *Onderwijs Beroep Arbeid, Postbus 829, AV Eindhoven, NL-5600.*

DETHERIDGE T., NCET, *Milburn Hill Road, Science Park, Coventry CV4 7JJ UK.*

DEUNFF J., Inspect. de l'Academie, Ed. Nationale, *3 rue Emile Raspail, F-94110 Arcueil.*

DUARTE J., *Escola Superior de Educaçao de Setubal, Nucleo de Tecnologia, Estrada das Santas, Estefanilha, 2910 Portugal.*

EM B., *Potters Green Primary School, Leicestershire, UK.*

ESCHBACH, *Min. for Ed. Nordrhein-Westfalen Volklinger Strasse 49, 40221 Dusseldorf.*

FIERMONTE, *Crauthem Primary School, Roeser, Luxembourg.*

FLETCHER C., *Imagination Tech., Bagshaw Hall, Bakewell, Derbyshire DE4 1DL, UK.*

GIRARDOT C., (IUFM de Creteil), *22 rue de la Fonte des Godets, Antony 94240, France.*

GRETSCH G., *Ministere de l'Education Nationale, 29 rue Aldringen, L-2926 Luxembourg.*

GUICHARD J., *La Villette - Cité des Enfants, 30 ave Corentin Cariou, 75019 Paris.*

HART B., *Imagination Technology, Bagshaw Hall, Bakewell, Derbyshire DE4 1DL, UK.*

HEMSLEY K., NCET, *Milburn Hill Road, Science Park, Coventry CV4 7JJ UK.*

HOWLETT F., NCET, *Milburn Hill Road, Science Park, Coventry CV4 7JJ UK.*

ISAKSSON T., *University College of Falun/Borlänge, Box 2004, S-791 02 Falun, Sweden.*

LAGAE F., CREADIM, *Ernest Claeslaan 8, B-3080 Tervuren, Belgium.*

LODINI E., *Dipartimento de Scienze dell'Educazione, Via Zamboni, 40126 Bologna.*

MATOS F., *Instit. de Inovaçao Educacional, rua Artilharia Um 105, P-1000 Lisbon.*

MORGAN J., NCET, *Milburn Hill Road, Science Park, Coventry CV4 7JJ UK.*

PAPROTTÉ W., ZERES, *Universitatsstrafe 142, D-44799 Bochum, Germany.*

PEETERS L., PRINT, *Onderwijs Beroep Arbeid, Postbus 829, 5600 AV Eindhoven.*

PÉPIN L., *Unité Européenne d'Eurydice, Rue d'Arlon 15 B-1050 Brussels.*

PICHAUT J-P., *Ministère de l'Ed. Nationale, 110 rue de Grenelle, 75357 Paris Cedex 07.*

QUIGLEY M., NCET, *Milburn Hill Road, Science Park, Coventry CV4 7JJ UK.*

RAMALHO-CORREIA A-M., INETI, *Azinhaga dos Lameiros à Estrada do Paço do Lumiar, Edificio A, P-1699 Lisboa Cedex.*

REIS CAMPOS M de F., *Rua do Carrascal, Lote 15-1°E, P-2725 Mem Martins, Portugal.*

RIVERS J., *Grendon Primary School, Northamptonshire, UK.*

SINKO M., *Koulun Tietotekniikkakeskus, Unikkotie 2C, 01300 Vantaa, Finland.*

SMART L., *Roehampton Institute, Digby Stuart College, London SW15 5PU.*

SOLA P-G., SCIENTER 3, *Via Val d'Aposo, Bologna, I-40122, Italy.*

Staff of LITTLE HILL PRIMARY SCHOOL, *Wigston, Leicestershire, UK.*

Staff of ST. CUTHBERTS PRIMARY SCHOOL, *Great Glen, Leicestershire, UK.*

THATCHER C., *Potters Green Primary School, Leicestershire, UK.*

TOFFOLA C. D., *Miistrero Della Pubblica Istruzione, Viale Trastevere, Rome, I-00100.*

TREMUTH F., *Altweis Primary School, Altweis, Luxembourg.*

VERPORTEN D., *14 rue du Prieuré, Louvain-la-Neuve, B-1348, Belgium.*

VIAUD J-B., *Association E.P.I., 13, rue du Jura, F-75013 Paris, France.*

VITELI J., *University of Tampere, P.O. Box 607, FIN-33101 Tampere, Finland.*

VITIELLO G., *Council of Europe Directorate of Ed. Culture & Sport, Strasbourg F-67075.*

WIRTGEN G., *ISERP, B.P. 2, L-7201, Walferdange, Luxembourg.*

WOESTMANN H., *Westfälische Wilhelms-Universität, Munster, Germany.*

WRIGHT J., NCET, *Milburn Hill Road, Science Park, Coventry CV4 7JJ UK.*

The future of this study depends on the contribution of primary school teachers using IT in their own class. We invite you to fill out the following grids to inform us of projects currently underway. Please send the completed documents to:

Editions ESKA

Réf : Ampère

5 avenue de l'Opéra

75001 Paris - France

BACKGROUND GRID

ID/COUNTRY:	
NAME OF PROJECT:	
DURATION:	
OBJECT:	
PROJECT DESCRIPTION:	
ORGANISATION:	
TEACHER TRAINING:	
USER'S COMMENTS:	
FUNDING:	
FORMAL EVALUATION:	
FURTHER READING:	
USEFUL ADDRESSES:	

On-site Observation

SCHOOL/CLASS:

DATE:

RELEVANCE OF IT:

PROGRAM USED:

COMPUTER DISTRIBUTION:

INTERACTION ALLOWED BY SOFTWARE:

VARIETY OF ACTIVITIES TAKING PLACE SIMULTANEOUSLY:

TEACHER PURPOSE (3 CULTURES):

GROUP WORK/TEAM SPIRIT:

SENSE OF RESPONSIBILITY/ PERSONAL DISCIPLINE:

DEGREE OF DECISION-MAKING/COMMITMENT/WILL INGNESS TO TAKE RISKS:

SENSE OF INITIATIVE/ CURIOSITY/CREATIVITY:

DEGREE OF ATOMISATION/ SOCIALISATION:

SENSE OF ACHIEVEMENT/ PRIDE IN WORK:

CORRESPONDENCE TO PURPOSE/LEVEL OF ACHIEVEMENT IN CULTURE:

Index

L O U I S - J E A N
avenue d'Embrun, 05003 GAP cedex
Tél. : 92.53.17.00
Dépôt légal : 785 — Octobre 1996
Imprimé en France